Doubting is Not Enough

Edgar N. Jackson and
Marshall E. Dimock

SCM PRESS LTD

334 01970 2

First published 1982
by SCM Press Ltd
58 Bloomsbury Street, London WC1

Typeset by Gloucester Typesetting Services
and printed in Great Britain by
Richard Clay Ltd (The Chaucer Press),
Bungay, Suffolk

Doubting is Not
Enough

Contents

Preface

History makes it clear that religion is a source of great power. It has done much to shape human history. Human consciousness needs some source for its values, its social goals and the security of group life. But these values are melded from the personal aspirations of individuals who have the gifts and responsibilities of human consciousness.

We two, who have lived long in the realm of idea, have had the benefit of years of retirement in rural Vermont where rumination on elemental things comes easily. Our paths have crossed and at their juncture we have paused and thought together. The product of some of our thinking is reflected in the pages that follow.

One of us has been a political scientist closely involved with every national administration over the last fifty years. Assigned by the American government, the United Nations, or in the course of his own research, to many countries and cultures abroad, a perspective has emerged that sees the relationship of value systems, political systems and human aspirations. Now free to speak unequivocally, issues are confronted and whatever wisdom the years have granted comes into sharp focus.

The other of us has brought together the insights of the personality sciences and the activities of the therapeutic community in hospital, clinic and religious activities. A pioneer in the pastoral care movement and the author of the first comprehensive textbook in the new discipline of crisis psychology, he melds parish, clinic, library and classroom in an effort to assess the problems and possibilities of humans in the last quadrant of the twentieth century.

Many fruitful and challenging hours have been spent together in exploring, assessing and interpreting our perspectives. We have become so close in spirit that we have difficulty in knowing the boundaries of our personal investment of thought and formulated words. We concur in what each other has written.

We freely admit that ours is a work in progress. While we are quite sure of our direction, we are willing to be marked by a healthy tentativeness as to some of the details. We give you what we have done with confidence, but also with a willingness to listen. We know that there are important areas that have not been touched. We are working on these. If time allows, we will offer our insights and suggestions on other matters in further works in process. We trust that these pages will seem more like conversations than like essays.

We are appreciative of the responses of people with whom we have shared our thinking. They have been encouraging by their responses which have said that our efforts were needed, relevant and reasonable and perhaps too long delayed.

So we welcome your responses to our shared thinking while we continue our ruminations in the midst of quiet hills that fill us with awe and wonder as they turn magenta, gold, purple and red. In this atmosphere, worship and wonder are united as are also, we hope, ruminating and relevance.

1 Permanence and Change

It is the central core of religion rather than its antiquity which accounts for its power and durability. It is a core which has many times demonstrated its ability to respond to the new and the challenging. We do not need a new religion for a new age, as some contend, but a clearer appreciation, based upon expanded knowledge, of what constitutes the central core that is universal.

In a time of worldwide revolution and threat of shortages and wars, survival is much on people's minds. Involved is not only physical survival but an acceptable way of life. Religion is central to this survival equation, because, whether it is a secular or a theistic religion, it is exposed to a common requirement: it must be relevant to men's needs and to their methods of solving pressing problems. Moreover, the relevance of religion is of two kinds: the immediate and the future. There is no good deluding ourselves with evanescent solutions if in a short time they are to prove futile.

Religion, in the universal sense of that term, is a never-ending search for truth and the unities that individuals and groups need if they are to have values and standards to live by. As such, religion is not a take-it-or-leave-it proposition, a badge that one wears on the Sabbath. It is an essential. An essential no matter what the name, the political system, or the social structure of institutions. Religion is something the individual uses every day and that affects every area of his life. It gives him inspiration and it gives him comfort. It is a belief and an ideal. In the intelligent life of the individual, it is the one thing that is universal. Political ideologies may come and go, but on analysis all are fractional. One stresses economic determinism, another monarchy or its antithesis, philosophical anarchy, another constitutions and forms of government. But seldom, if ever, does an ideology approach the level of religion as integrator and unifier of all strands and interests of life.

It is in this durable but evolutionary sense that we intend to deal with religion's role today. Our assumption is that all religious truth could not possibly be delivered at any one time, but that even if the theology were unshakable, the modifications of structure and application to new needs is constantly occurring. Concentration on the real maintains the foundations of religion. Religion also has a deep concern for the future and the inevitability of change.

In what follows, therefore, we deal with the core of religion and its eternal truths, temporal as well as divine, with religion's morals and ethics, which are not separate but of a piece, with the ideal and the actual, the role of prophecy, sin and salvation, and immortality. Prominent attention is given to the problems of suffering and health. The aspirations of hope, joy and peace are also part of the compound. We suggest that Jesus' teaching has far more relevance to the world's problems today than much of what is now called Christian doctrine. Running through all this is the idea of consciousness, the connecting link between the origin of life and its growth into an unfolding and almost limitless potential.

There are three main reasons why religion may be the most important interest of human beings. The first has been mentioned: religion is the only interest of man that deals comprehensively with the inter-relations of life from which unity may proceed. It provides identity, in the sense of personality and character, for the individual and for the larger groups of which he is a part.

Secondly, religion is the only interest that combines all attempts to discover the source, evolution and destiny of life. Man seems to need this knowledge if he is to attain true selfhood. Moreover, the better he acquires it, the better able he is to develop his potential and his deepest satisfactions. Religion is based on the assumption that there must have been an original architect and that the world has cause-and-effect relationships, commonly called 'laws', which it follows. Scientists concerned with the philosophy of science and social scientists concentrating on the philosophy of the state approach the main interest of the theologian at this same point.

The third reason for religion's distinctive and transcendent importance is its concern with values. Values are the basis of constitutions, human rights, the rule of law, civilized behaviour and most of the other interests that people seek while trying to better their lot. Most of technological technique automatically neglects values: religion restores the balance. Or, in another area, happiness is more qualitative than quantitative: religion helps to keep it that way.

Because religion is integrative, its functional utility depends upon its ability to keep pace with change, which some call the only constant. Even if all religions were 'revealed' at one time – say two thousand years ago – this alone would not be sufficient to guarantee permanence and relevance – the world has changed too much. Religion has always been partly revealed and partly evolutionary. It expands to meet new situations. It grows by incorporating some of the greatest thoughts of some of the greatest minds that the world has produced from the time of Socrates and Confucius. Some of the best of it is sheer poetry, even though, in some cases, written by scientists who are supposed to be prosaic.

When religion fails to grow, then contradictions and even paradoxes sometimes appear. Religion's basic tenets may be true, but its failure to adjust to change may make the applications of these truths less than true. As in other areas of life, people may lose sight of the original objective and focus only on the form, the veneer. Or take another example: religion is by nature universal, but in the name of religion the tribes of mankind may try to decimate other tribes, although they both believe in God. Rather than reject religion, however, because crimes have been committed in its name, or because sometimes it has been used as the opiate of the people, its larger utility is such that it is the better part of wisdom to try to clarify its meanings, to search for universals and to bring ends and means into working accord, while not neglecting its failures to keep up with change and to remain relevant.

When religion fails, or people turn against its institutional expositor, the church, then, as has happened several times in recent world history, the common tendency is to turn to the political state as the synthesizer of belief and aspiration. This immediately tends to create a nationalistic bias. It also associates aspiration with the nature of the state, which of necessity uses force and coercion to enforce its laws. Hence, where religion is voluntary, attachment to the ideology of the state becomes coercive, and where religion is universal, the state, even under the best of circumstances, takes a narrower focus. A third result is that secular rule quite naturally focuses on ethics – witness, for example, the wide use made of the term 'socialist ethics' by communist countries – and, as we shall see in chapter 3 where ethics is discussed, ethics is of lesser scope than religion and is derived from it. A fourth factor is of even greater importance: if religion is not considered a universal body of knowledge binding people together spiritually and providing the basis for their selfhood and reasons for living, it is futile to look elsewhere in life for a force that is capable of promoting and maintaining world peace. For even international law, as its founder Hugo Grotius, the Dutchman, was the first to recognize in the seventeenth century, is essentially a matter of morality. The biologist might say, 'All religions belong to the same genus.' Hence, as elsewhere in the field of knowledge, a careful reading of another's religious beliefs may sometimes enrich one's own beliefs without threatening or displacing them.

Knowledge in some areas has greatly increased, especially in the physical and social sciences; and applying these findings to the original core of religion often has an enriching consequence. To search constantly for these enrichments of knowledge and insight shows no disrespect for the original teachings because, to a remarkable degree, the writings of great minds gladly accept the essence and build around it. An example of this is Ralph Waldo Emerson's insistence that real religion is the individual's direct communication with God; that God and nature are one and the same; that everything in nature is moral; that goodness and beauty are inherent in nature and become blemished only as man is calloused and uncomprehending. Emerson subscribed to Plato's doctrine:

> Let us declare the cause which led the Supreme Ordainer to produce and compose the universe. He was good; and he who is good has no kind of envy. Exempt from envy, he wished all things should be as much as possible like himself. Whosoever, taught by wise men, shall admit to this as the prime cause of the origin and foundation

of the world, will be in truth. All things are for the sake of the good, and it is the cause of every thing beautiful.

It is this positive, up-beat view of religion that people everywhere cherish. People want a faith that is so pervasive that they can live by it every day. They want to know where they came from, where they stand in relation to total experience and reality and where they are going. They want a reasoned combination of intellect and feeling that will make them feel whole and important in a world that is fractured and increasingly artificial. They want values that are comprehensive enough to include church and state in the same intellectual concept. They want faith in themselves so they can have faith in others. They want to act from inspiration instead of fear, because they suffer from too many kinds of anxieties as it is.

A religion such as we have been describing could hardly be used for the purposes which sceptical intellectuals frequently object to and which causes them to break with religion. Religion could not become authoritarian: it has strongly held beliefs but focuses on universals and the search for truth. It is idealistic but realistic at the same time. It elevates intellect but accords equal status to values and humane sentiments. It is opposed to cynicism because it is wasteful. It believes in the possibility that much truth may exist which has not yet been discovered. It believes that ends and means are intellectually and morally inseparable. It believes that attitudes of superiority are an offence against God. It believes that power is 'with', not 'over'. It distrusts institutions because it realizes that they are means, not ends. It appreciates that institutions, like individuals, constantly need to be 'renewed' as they become myopic and self-centred instead of humane. It holds that memory should focus on the good and not on the failures and disappointments of life. It recognizes that forgiveness strengthens the giver as well as the receiver. It believes that the ultimate reality is consciousness, which may be described as a force which gave primitive life its energy and potential and is present everywhere in the universe today, promoting communication, understanding and bonds of spiritual vitality extending even beyond the death of the individual.

According to this view, theology is subject to the same intellectual requirements as the rest of knowledge: it must be true, relevant, testable. It must be verified by experience. It should become the common property of mankind and not be considered the disputatious arena of academic infighting. The common criticism, therefore, is that theology does not say enough about the *universals* of religion. It is vague about God, for example, or assumes there are 'chosen' people. Secondly, theology needs to say more about the *core* of religion, the part that is permanent. Thirdly, it should seek spirit and truth and realize that *form* and ritual frequently dominate and weaken it rather than serve essential goals. Modern man also wants more attention paid to practical *morals* and *ethics*, which a bewildering complexity makes imperative, or otherwise theology may be weakened as these applications of religion are taken over by other groups. It expects religious leaders to exercise a *prophetic* role, because only seers can prevent collective blindness. It requires religion to be the *censor* of the political state and economic power groups because religion or its lack expresses itself pragmatically in these areas more often than in churches and temples. It wants creativity in the form of *inspiration* and synthesis. But above all else, it seeks international understanding and *peace*.

Religion must communicate. It is a one-to-one relationship between the worshipper and the creator. Everyone is a religious teacher who practises religion. One sex has as much responsibility as the other. Holy men and women are venerated not because of their position in a hierarchy but because they are seers and set outstanding examples.

It is admittedly a challenging job description. But if its main outlines could be made to work, the clouds of pessimism would be driven away by the energies which appear like the coming of spring every year.

2 The Core of Religion

At the heart of religious truth is a vital force which, like an endless belt, explains creation, growth, decay and renewal. This vital force becomes a communication system between the soul of man and the oversoul at the centre of the universe, which people everywhere call the creator. The vital force operates through laws of creation, growth and survival and through a spirit which results when that vital force forms connections between man, God and nature to develop spirit and values.

The laws and spirit complement each other to form a unity, as do intellect and sentiment. God never dies and is as much alive today as in the beginning. Everything in the universe is alive, interacting and has potential. The potential is inherent in the vital force and takes the form of consciousness, which is the clue to the life cycle and life after death.

Life is governed by an understanding of the laws and vital forces existing in creation and by a partnership between man and God, in which each assumes responsibilities. Renewal is inherent in God and nature, but suffers when man does not fully comprehend the laws of the universe and hence does not cooperate. The same is true of decay, which is the chief source of lowered vitality, but which is inherent in the scheme of things. Renewal takes place more effectively when the organism stays close to the original vital force, which is to say God.

Religion may be defined as both the knowledge and the practice of the intellectual and spiritual relation between man, God and nature, which results in beliefs which command man's highest affections and loyalties and by which people judge all other areas of life.

The soul may be defined as the nucleus, located in the area of the brain which contains the vital force with which three things happen: the individual gets his personality and spirit from it; he communicates with God; and it is the basis of his immortality.

By vital force is meant the energy which apparently existed even before the earth was formed and which has a dynamism that is somewhat independent of structure and which, because of its inherent potential, is apparently capable of specialization, creativity and survival after death.

Nature consists of everything in the known universe and beyond, it all being part of a unity which God created. Through all this universe, there are vital forces which connect one's soul with the souls of others and with the soul of God. As part of this unity, the diverse fields of physics, biology, chemistry, mathematics, psychology, engineering and medicine have increasingly been drawn together in the form of the philosophy of science and tend to confirm this broad view of nature. Thus the vital force of which we speak has reality, is sometimes perceived as identifiable, and not only explains higher communications, but may also provide the clue to the origin of life. Life may have started with something that might be the origin of the soul and that is why the soul is imperishable.

The laws of the universe are those which have parallels in various aspects of research. The laws of biology having to do with individuation (specialization) and group solidarity (cohesion), for example, are no different than those found in the social sciences. And when physics asserts that energy is never lost, but merely takes another form, or that many things (including the earth) would blow up if they were not kept sufficiently in balance, the analogy to this is found in Aristotle's belief that one extreme in social life begets the other extreme and that continuity therefore depends upon balance. When religion calls these moral laws, instead of physical laws, closer examination will reveal that they have the same intellectual roots. In both cases, God, working through man, is the author. When we call them moral, it is often because they have high survival value.

God is the oversoul with which man communicates and whose presence unifies the world. He is the source of the vital force and hence of everything else discussed here, such as creation, growth,

8

decay and renewal. He made the universe according to a rational plan, otherwise it seems unlikely that the laws of the universe would be so reliable – and they are marvellously reliable. It seems likely, also, that God intended that there should be an element of chance (which philosophers of science puzzle over) because chance may be due to a number of causes: the complexity of variables, a disjunction between time and event, human error or caprice, or the challenge chance frequently provides. God is the intellect that makes everything in nature complementary: truth and beauty, goodness and truth, goodness and beauty.

Communication takes many forms. One of them is prayer. Another is worship. As we communicate with God, our sense of consciousness grows and also our sense of wonder and inner contentment. A person has mystical experiences, which may be defined as being fully absorbed in a reflective state where communication of spirit and vitality occurs. Such a person also has peak experiences, which are described by Abram Maslow, the humanist psychologist, as an exalted and exultant feeling which makes one feel so inspired and elevated that the memory lasts a lifetime. If, in individual or group religion, mystical, extra-sensory experiences are not present, there is something vitally wrong. At times, in the communication between God and man and communion with one's self and with others, a person should become aware of a vital connective force. After such experiences, the soul and its radiations become increasingly intellectually convincing and are increasingly present in one's consciousness.

Unity may be defined as the combination of opposites to constitute a natural whole. Or, in a larger sense, it is the knowledge of how all aspects of life fit together and interact to maintain life and balance. From a psychological standpoint, everyone seems to need a certain unity in order to be socially and personally effective. Unity becomes the basis of inspiration. The scientist finds his centre in nature, the farmer in his land, the technologist in his machines, the scholar in his books, the artist in his vision, the statesman in his philosophy, the businessman in his enterprises, the child in his or her dreams, Ralph Waldo Emerson in a drop of dew. All of these, to be sure, are lesser goals, but all of them are related in one way or another to the idea of God. God is intelligence, beauty and goodness combined in a unity and fused by a consciousness or vital force that is everywhere pervasive.

Consciousness is intensified insight and awareness, a sense of being connected with the oversoul. It is a combination of things: the vital force, the energy which comes churning through the mind and the spirit; a feeling of closeness to reality; the gift of extra-sensory perception, an ability which some have to communicate over long distances. The best hope of finding out more about God than men have learned over many centuries is by pushing back the veil that has long inhibited consciousness research.

Where does man fit in this list of key terms? If nature is defined as Emerson did, namely as everything in the known universe, including man, then it is doubtful if man comes through very well. For Emerson was clearly right when he argued that the natural state, created by God, is good, moral and beautiful. When it becomes markedly otherwise, it is unfortunately man who is the main culprit. This, in itself, should cause man to be more modest than he is and it helps to explain the biblical statement, 'the meek shall inherit the earth'. Because man has so many shortcomings to acknowledge, it seems presumptious to contend, as some have, that God is made in the image of man instead of the other way around. It would be more comely if mankind understood that a more feasible goal is to make man human. But by following natural law.

A respect in which animals are frequently superior to humans is in their intuitive faculties. Much remains to be learned about this intuitive ability and its connection with the larger question of consciousness. But there must be some connection. Numerous examples of this intuitive capacity might be mentioned: dogs are frequently better judges of character than humans and they seem to know it instinctively. Hours before a major storm is approaching in northern New England, the chickens know it and the humans do not. Similarly, in the summer, cows in the pasture lie down several hours before a storm approaches. Or still another example: trout that are fed daily by the same person will respond much more slowly, if at all, when fed by a stranger. Every time we learn more about animal and human nature, we learn more about theology.

What is the role of myth in the search for the core of religion?

Myth is something that is believed although its truth may not have been proved and hence its thought content is taken wholly or partly on faith. Some myths serve useful purposes, but it cannot be questioned that humans become more developed and enriched in selfhood and effectiveness when myth can be superseded by rational belief and fully tested in the actual experiences of life.

Unless one is content to accept religious teaching on the basis of faith, as it is handed down from one generation to the next in many cultures, it becomes a matter of some importance to inquire how one goes about validating some of the core ingredients discussed here. Take prayer, for example, or extra-sensory perception.

The best way to test the core ingredients of religion is to conduct your own tests. Much may be learned about some things, of course, by reading the results of reliable research. This is true, especially, for the ideas of the biologists, geneticists, psychologists and philosophers of science we have referred to earlier. It also applies to the difficult but promising field of research into consciousness and transcendentalism, which may be the new frontier of religion as well as of science.

But, in most areas, there is no substitute for making one's own applications. We have discovered, for example, that the oftener we pray and the more consistently, the better the channels of communication open up to us. The sincerity and nature of the communication is another variable. Further, there are times when the feeling of being in communion with something 'out there' is much stronger or weaker than at other times, causing one to wonder why. When the communication is good, one feels composed and happy, new ideas and worthwhile ventures are often suggested, everything seems to be all right and one feels humbler and more self-confident at the same time.

This might suggest that possibly the virtue of professing religion is not its truth or independent beneficient powers, but the psychological stance of the supplicant. In other words, if one studies and ponders, takes a serious view of life and is unselfish and dedicated, but professes no religion, perhaps this is why religion 'works' with so many people. It may be the attitude rather than the belief. Thus, it might be argued that it does not matter what religion one subscribes to, or what one considers the core of religion, the communicant would feel satisfied and fulfilled simply by dedication and long practice.

There are, to be sure, varieties of religious experience, as William James clearly demonstrated. Also, it cannot be questioned that dedicated and unselfish persons develop common unselfish traits whether their focus is church or civic oriented. But, beyond this, two things seem true and worth stressing. The first is that different religions seem to produce differing results on personality and behaviour. And secondly, it seems equally true that when the religious person discovers the core of his religious belief and the core is supported by the best research the human mind has been able to produce, the consequences are as favourable as when animals, such as deer, live in accordance with the laws of survival and maximum advantage.

Does a person have a duty to become religious and attend church? Yes, if it does not violate his intellect. Should he accept the authority of the church fathers? The answer is the same. But if the individual comes to religion voluntarily and as a result of his own thinking and feeling, the results are always better, for him and for religion itself. It is better for the church because, as religion becomes institutionalized, it experiences inevitably the same difficulty from which all other institutions suffer: the church tends to become bureaucratized, it seeks power and wealth; it measures success in quantative rather than qualitative terms; it gradually stresses lesser things, such as ritual, rather than the major objects it did in the beginning. All of these dangers can be avoided or corrected, if there is enough awareness of the problem in advance.

To summarize, we believe in God, in the soul, in an orderly universe, in a nature that is good and beautiful. Life for man would be better, now and in the future, if he understood more fully the laws and spirit of the universe, which it is the function of religion to lay forth and constantly update.

These ideas have been expressed poetically and with Emerson's usual picturesque language when he said,

There is one soul.
It is related to the world.
Art is its action thereon.

Science finds its methods.

Literature is its record.

Religion is the emotion of reverence that it inspires.

Ethics is the soul illustrated in human life.

Society is the finding of this soul by individuals in each other.

Trades are the learning of the soul in nature by labor.

Politics is the activity of the soul illustrated by power.

Manners are silent and mediate expressions of soul.

And again,

The world is not the product of manifold power, but of one will, of one mind.

That will is everywhere active. Whatever opposes that will is everywhere balked and baffled.

Good is positive. Evil is like cold, which is the privation of heat.

So much benevolence as a man has, so much life hath he, for benevolence is real and not transitory.

All things proceed out of the same spirit, which is differently named love, justice, temperance.

Emerson concludes by saying that if a man follows the good, he prospers, but if he follows selfishness and greed, he withers and dies. The reason behind all this is that God has made laws of the universe. The highest law is the spirit of good running through all life. Hence, if a person seeks good ends, he will survive and find happiness, but if he fails to heed God's laws, his seed will become as a 'mote', a mere trace of what it was.

If we put ourselves in the hands of God, will he take care of us? Yes, we believe he will. But it is exceedingly important to analyze just how this divine guidance may be expected to take place. There are two views about this. One of them holds that the individual has no part in ruling his own life because, if he is willing to become passive and inert, God will provide. In other words, it is God who makes our daily moves and takes all our decisions and we are like a leaf being moved along by the flow of a mountain stream. For a recluse, a person who sits and ponders day and night, this is doubtless a satisfactory solution.

The alternative, which we like better, takes a different form. It holds that God establishes the laws of life and growth, of regression, and renewal and decay, but that he expects us, having intelligence and the ability to attune ourselves to his nature and spirit, to take the responsibility for managing our own lives.

3 Human Values and Politics

Because there is one God and everything in life is inter-related, it follows that theology and political philosophy have the same source and share the same basic principles. In the American Declaration of Independence, the framers used the term 'eternal truths' and even the stronger one, 'self-evident truths'. The framers were, in effect, trying to bring into practical working relationship their mystical assumptions about the nature of man and their perception of a government that could give expression to these ideas about the sacredness of life, the need for freedom to develop it and the necessity to set forth, boldly and clearly, principles derived from higher sources and incorporated into written constitutions.

How does one move back in time and circumstance to try to capture again some of the mood and meaning of this original struggle with values and their practical application? A visit to the House of Burgesses, in Williamsburg, once the capital of Virginia, gives one a sense of what these values might be. Here one senses the efforts to bring together two traditions that were always related, though not always comfortably, the theological and the political concepts of the nature of man.

These Virginia legislators were literate men. Many were educated in the classics. They would not have been total strangers to the ringing words of Sophocles, 'Nor did I reckon thine august decree of so much force that mortals for its sake should dare transgress the unwritten laws of God, those laws unfailing, immemorial and immortal.' As always, these laws of God are unspecified though universally acknowledged, undefined although constantly assumed. Their familiarity with Plato's *Republic* might well have made it possible for them to talk of freedom while they held slaves.

The Virginia legislators were the better-off people in the colony, the landed gentry, the plantation owners. They were not insensitive to human values even though they were gripped in a system that exploited humans. The seeds of moral concern had already been planted by the gentle voices of men like John Woolman, who warned that they would never be truly free while they enslaved other men.

Quite in contrast was the mood of Thomas Paine. In those times that tried the souls of men, he championed the rights of man. Some who have studied the text of the Declaration of Independence feel that the words and phrases therein have more of Thomas Paine echoing through them than the philosophy of Thomas Jefferson (who became the third president of the United States and its leading spokesman for democratic ideals). Those who made up the bulk of the revolutionary army were men who did their own sweating, cleared their own land and hoed their own corn.

The ideas of humanity and freedom, espoused by both the landed gentry and the hewers of wood and drawers of water, were not easily put into words. Rather, they were felt as assumptions or viewed in mystical terms. The full impact of this type of sensitivity to a value system comes alive if one spends May Day, the international day of revolution, behind the Iron Curtain. On a recent May Day in Bratislava, loudspeakers blanketed the city with raucous sound interspersed with martial music. The air was shattered with manipulative political sounds. The noise was accented by the evidence of security, with pairs of machine-gun laden soldiers patrolling the streets constantly. The contrast of political repression with individual freedom was accented in the public park where thousands gathered to observe and share in the traditional dances. In beautiful provincial costumes, the dancers expressed the mood of light-hearted freedom and the joy of living to the lilting Bohemian music. One does not easily feel the mood of freedom until it emerges from an active contrast with restraint and repression.

In one sense, all political systems operate from a theological base. That is, if we assume a theology emerges from an interaction between a concept of the nature of the human being and a concept of the nature of the universe as cosmic law and order, to which the human must respond in order to fulfil destiny. In moving from one side of the Iron Curtain to the other, one senses the different ideas of the nature of people as people, and a social order that was state-oriented rather than person-centred.

In their efforts to establish a political system that was resonant to human needs as well as political necessity, those who founded the American republic rested their assumptions heavily on the truths they held to be self-evident. But because they were political pioneers, their claims had an experimental and tentative quality. To build a system on moral grandeur required moral sensitivity on the part of the mass of individuals who supported the audacious experiment. This was not always easy. The first major responsibility of the new government was to control the land manipulators who abused their freedom in order to exploit.

At the higher levels of political concern, there was the conflict between sound principle and sound currency. In the dramatic conflict between Aaron Burr and Alexander Hamilton, this struggle found lethal expression. The Hamiltonian Federalists emphasized elitism and a mercantilist policy, whereas the Jeffersonian Republicans favoured populism and pastoral ways of life. The fear was that the elitists would return to a monarchism and let the goals of revolution fall into compromise. Strong feelings produced strong words. Aaron Burr, the vice-president of the United States, challenged the integrity of Hamilton and a duel ensued. It was not until the Smithsonian Institution obtained the historic pistols in 1975 to make duplicates for the bicentennial celebration that the perfidy of Hamilton was at last brought to light, more than 170 years later. The Smithsonian found that the pistols had been tampered with so that Hamilton's had an eight ounce trigger pressure while Burr's had a twelve pound trigger pressure. When the nervous Hamilton pulled his trigger too soon, he cried out that he had not meant to shoot his adversary. Thus Hamilton became the symbol of nobility and martyrdom, while Burr was accused of murder and was never again a vital political influence in the United States. The impact of Hamilton's long-concealed deception was to win sympathy for his policies, which, to this day, have been the major influence on the business and economic life of the United States.

The deeply rooted conflict between things and people, sound fiscal policy and human needs has persisted through the years. In times of crisis, human values are sacrificed to economic necessity. In the late 1970s, this conflict produced a conservative movement with Margaret Thatcher's premiership emphasizing fiscal restraint in spite of human needs, quite like the taxpayers revolt in the United States. Human needs and social values are sacrificed to the claims of property. When the taxes of one of the authors of this book were raised and he wrote to the selectmen (councillors for the rural communities of New England) to congratulate them in their belated concern for more adequate schools and the children who could not speak for themselves, one of the selectmen visited him and said that it was the first letter of its kind they had ever received. And word got around and some of his neighbours suggested his sanity might have lapsed. Yet in this part of upper Appalachia where functional illiteracy is over eighty per cent, property claims still take precedence over human needs.

The mood of denial and affirmation that existed among the founding fathers of the United States has been a consistent theme through the years. The self-evident truths concerning people have often been compromised when property and its security have been in jeopardy. The original debate continues, with idealism and human grandeur mixed with exploitation and human degradation.

War stands as the most brutal evidence of the precedence of material values over human rights. The early casualties in war are truth and free exercise of opposition. Emotion takes priority over reason. The neutron bomb is a graphic example for it is deployed to destroy people without damaging property. As war becomes more impersonal, the problem becomes more acute. In the American Revolution, people confronted people and the personal element was a constant. Now, with pushbutton controls activating computers, the human dimension becomes more remote and raw power may not respond to the demands of reason.

When the focus on human needs is lost, human values tend to deteriorate. Alexander Solzhenitsyn, speaking at a Harvard University commencement ceremony, decried the loss of moral concerns and spoke eloquently of the decay of American ethical principles. Perhaps we needed this admonition, but it is only half of the picture. We can admit the wave of lawlessness and the loss of values in high places, but we can also question Solzhenitsyn's real knowledge of the American character and his appreciation for the underlying integrity and commitment of the American people.

The concerns that he focused on were the concerns of the American national tradition. How can we build a society that shows proper respect for human aspirations on the one hand and national and material security on the other? There are no simple or easy answers, but to deny that the struggle for answers does not exist is to fail to understand the genius of the democratic process at work. To fall prey to the assumption that power must always be met by power is to abandon alternatives and revert to the value system of those we would challenge. There must be a better way.

When we talk about freedom, justice and the rights of people, we are really looking at mystical concepts and religious concerns. The creator's endowment cannot be enforced by raw material power. It challenges us with something of a higher nature. This is the point where the concept of the unique and sacred nature of the human must remain central. Theology at the personal and social level emerges when the nature of the human is brought into active relationship with the realities of the external cosmic order. This is where theology and politics meet. This is where the balance of apparently conflicting value systems must be melded. Until the nature of the human quest is made compatible with theological and political concepts, there will be unrelenting conflict. Until the concept of the law and order of the universe is faced up to by both theology and politics, we will continue to have deception, ecological stress and environmental disaster.

How can these apparently conflicting interests be brought into a working unity? Not easily. We may be the first generation in human history that has the psychological insight and the cosmological perspective to bring these ideas into a comfortable working relationship. This appears to be the central problem we must face before we begin to resolve the other personal, national and international problems that confront us.

The first step in the direction of resolution of this deeply-rooted conflict is an altered state of perspective and a heightened consciousness of the role that each of us plays in the creating of a value system that balances human and property rights, people and things. When

America celebrated its two hundredth birthday, we were strong on flags but uncertain about the fables that had crept into our national history. We were strong on self-glorification but timid about self-examination. We made much of externals but avoided the painful responsibilities of looking openly at our behaviour and the value system that produced the behaviour.

If we are to mobilize the resources needed to create a revitalized sense of values, we will not do it by ignoring the need for values. We are quick to mobilize the things that have to do with external threats, as in a defence alert, for example. We should now be equally quick to confront the weaknesses of our internal climate, the place where our values grow. These, too, are times that try men's souls. Unless we are worthy of our inheritance as those who seek a system that can bring people and property, things and values, into a working relationship, we are failing our responsibility in a time of great need.

To do our share to verify the self-evident truths that our political and social ancestors proclaimed, we must have a heightened sense of the value of life, the importance of freedom for developing that life and the rights of people everywhere to seek personal fulfilment.

4 Religion and Morals

The source of morality is in the idea of a caring God, an idea which translates into concern for others – their needs, aspirations and values. Morality is based on that part of religion which stresses values. As shown in the preceding chapter, the political state relies upon eternal truths when it promotes moral beliefs and conduct. The chief values involved in moral conduct are caring for others, having respect for life, acting with probity and honour and having a sense of obligation which is inner-centred rather than coerced.

Morality may therefore be defined as a code of belief and conduct, centred in intellect and affections, which encourages individuals and groups to act public-spiritedly to promote the mutual needs, aspirations and values of others in a reciprocal relationship. The source of morals is religion. Ethics is the application of morals, or morals in action.

Morality, like religion, is something that grows at the centre of human existence. It is not something brought in from the outside. The social origin of unselfish concern for others' needs, aspirations and values, is the family. Caring for the young expands into a growing circle of relationships, to include relatives, communities, nations and eventually world population.

In the competition between traditional religions and the newer political ideologies (which are, in effect, secular religions), the outcome is still uncertain. Officially the world's largest population, the mainland Chinese, who constitute about a quarter of the population of the world, claim to be devoid of any theistic religion and attempt to extirpate even Confucianism. Similarly, in China's next-door neighbour, Soviet Russia, the official doctrine of the party in power is atheism. The U.S.S.R. has the second largest economic system in the world and, with a territorial size that is double that of the continental United States, seems to have great potential for growth. Anti-religion is also spreading to other areas of the world as well – to South-east Asia and more recently to Africa, for example. Inside all these countries, there are still, of course, thousands of secret believers in so-called orthodox faiths, and in the U.S.S.R. there is some evidence that religious tolerance is increasing rather than otherwise. But to add to the total competitiveness of secular influence, there is now no question that in traditionally Christian countries, such as Italy and France, the influence of secular beliefs is growing while conventional religious beliefs are losing ground. There have been conversations for some time, for example, between communist theorists and Christian theologians in these countries, who are seeking areas of possible agreement between the competing belief systems.

Suppose, at some time in the future, religion were to lose most of its theological support and would then have to fall back on a combination of morals and ethics as regulators of a people's lexicon of right and wrong? There seems to be no question that in any nation – no matter how extreme or how conservative its political ideology – there is an inescapable need of standards of some kind to regulate moral and ethical conduct. By this is meant rules concerning such matters as murder, theft, rape, assassination, corruption in high office, abortion, divorce, responsibility for the rearing of children, property rights and civil liberties. This also includes freedom from arrest at night and being hauled off to prison.

There is, of course, the law; and every country, no matter how concentrated its political domination or how irreligious its official creed, finds it necessary to have a body of law to regulate proper and improper conduct and thus discovers the need to make moral judgments. Sometimes these regimes, as ruthless and bloodthirsty as they seem to outside observers, have rigid rules for their citizens that can only be described as puritanical. In such countries, they use the word 'correct' more frequently than we do in the Western world and the term leaves no room for deviation or tolerance. One possible way of solving the paradox of choice between secular and theistic solutions, therefore, is to rely largely or almost entirely upon the legal code of the country for standards of proper conduct.

But even if one so concludes – and we do not – this still leaves unresolved the larger question of which the role of law is merely a part. How necessary is theological belief to a sound system of morals?

The political state cannot be expected to supercede religion for any extended period of time because of the inherent nature of government. It represents concentrated power, coercion by force, susceptibility to domination by an elite or an oligarchy and hence the use of amoral methods to achieve fractional goals. The church, as institution, is exposed to some of these same human weaknesses, too, but religion has an existence independent of any church organization and hence retains the vital force to transcend the shortcomings of institutions.

It is possible, of course, so to structure morality in government that the chances of its goals and objectives remaining moral are greatly increased. Some of the best methods are to increase citizen education, provide for free elections, maintain the balance between the executive and legislative branches, preserve an independent judiciary and administer the government through a dedicated corps of civil servants whose ruling motive is adherence to the larger good. In the United States, today, the greatest of these structural needs is the independent and principled stance of its administrative and judicial officials.

Law and government have their limits. Much of the difficulty the United States has been experiencing with agitating issues such as Watergate, Vietnam and loss of confidence in popular government – to mention the most obvious – is due to the fact that we have failed so far to develop a morality based upon a reconstructed theology. It might be possible for a nation to survive without a theology, but if it does have a theology that is relevant and sound, a country is much more firmly based with it than without it.

Ralph Waldo Emerson, with whose views we are in general agreement, at one point in his writing makes a distinction between God and nature and concludes that the view of God as being above and apart from the world actually produces a lower level of morality than Emerson's view, holding that God and nature are one, and that nature is inherently spiritual, moral and contains a natural discipline which inclines man to moral conduct. Ideals and perfection are inherent in nature and if man learns to understand and follow the principles of nature, he will become moral in the highest sense of that term. In other words, it is not the political state and its system of law, nor God and the orthodox idea that all rules and prohibitions are to be found in the Bible, that makes man moral. The rules and the prohibitions can go only so far. But not far enough to provide for the needs of modern man. Our morality must come from sources anterior to law and the authority of the political state. Otherwise modern man cannot develop codes of conduct adequate for dealing with the problems he now faces. We agree with this view.

Morality is sometimes defined as knowing the difference between right and wrong. Philosophers have traditionally dealt with the subject under two headings, duty and virtue. Duty takes the form of rules, derived from some authoritative source, such as religion or the law that everyone is supposed by customary or government-enforced standards to obey. Virtue, on the other hand, has a more subjective quality. It is more personalized. It is the fitting thing to do, whether required by duty and legal sanctions, or not. These two categories help to explain the scriptures and religious teaching.

There are three principal ways in which duty and virtue are unified and made a single body of knowledge. One is to see both branches of morality as originating with God; there are laws of the universe and there is a higher law of the universe which takes the form of spirit. The second source is philosophy, which may either be an off-shoot of theology, as St Gregory and St Francis and other church fathers conceived it when attempting to combine Christian and Platonic doctrines, or philosophy may be understood, as it has been for the most part since the Reformation, as man's attempt to synthesize all fields of knowledge and discover what principles are common to all of them. The third source is what are called 'the moral sentiments', which is the term that the authors of *Roget's Thesaurus* and dictionary editors apply to moral teaching, whether religious or secular.

If one turns to the Bible for moral teaching, one is impressed by the degree to which the Old Testament stresses duty and rules. Equally, when one turns to the New Testament, the main impression is that morality is based upon virtue and spirit. Jesus said, and clearly meant, that he did not come to change the law but only to give it effect and breathe more love and charity into the teachings of his Jewish predecessors. What he was clearly trying to do was to restore the balance between rules and voluntarism, which he interpreted, and doubtless rightly, as God's intent. J. B. Phillips, in his *The New Testament in Modern English* (Macmillan 1965), explains this as follows (p 551):

> The Pharisees (whom Jesus was constantly upbraiding) were a class of zealous Jews whose chief characteristic lay in their separation from the heathen and from all that they considered evil. They were the Puritans of their day, and emphasized the spiritual rather than the nationalistic side of Judaism. We might fairly say that they were Churchmen rather than statesmen. And, again, though there were good men among them, they tended to concentrate upon rigid observances, to the exclusion of human sympathy and under-standing. It was this tendency, and the conviction that they alone were right, which brought them into conflict with Jesus.

Another difference between the Old and New Testaments is that Old Testament writers constantly emphasized God in the burning bush, on the mountaintop, or in his bolts of lightning, whereas Jesus dealt almost exclusively with the appearance of God in people. This is why many writers have said, and doubtless correctly, that the New Testament is essentially a 'social' gospel; that is, the rules and spirit which should guide human beings in their quest for religious spirit and reality.

The clearest illustration of the difference is found in a comparison of the Ten Commandments as found in Exodus and the Beatitudes as found in Matthew 5. The Ten Commandments are largely 'thou shalt not's and deal with killing, stealing, adultery, bearing false witness, covetousness and graven images. Only three have a positive note: honour God, the Sabbath and your parents. All of these ten are patently important rules that enter into man's formulation of morals and morality.

Consider, however, what a different range of subjects Jesus chose to emphasize in the Beatitudes: the poor in spirit, the mourners, the meek, the righteous, the merciful, the pure in heart, the peacemakers, those who are persecuted for righteousness' sake and those against whom all kinds of evil is said because of their support of his ministry. Clearly, most of these – the first seven, especially – were positive statements, emphasizing values and virtue and not being much concerned with 'thou shalt not's. Jesus realized the psychological truth that positive motivation often produces more lasting results than the inculcation of fear.

Almost every major commentator on television remarks at one time or another that some new and hard thinking about morals is needed in the United States. This is not explained merely by the Watergate, Lockheed and Korean influence scandals. Deeper causes directly affect the family, the economy and crimes against persons and property. A few writers – the ones who deal with discontinuities – find the explanation of the decline in morality in the emergence of new offences for which there are no ancient rules. Others are content to state that if modern man obeyed all the injunctions in the Bible, the number of 'new' derelictions of duty and violations of virtue would be few and manageable. Still others contend that the old rules have been violated for so long that even people who are deeply commited to religious values are confused and consequently become inconsistent.

Long before prohibition, American governments already had a long tradition of trying to legislate morality. This took the form of the so-called Blue Laws regulating drinking habits, Sunday closing and the like, aimed at protecting morals as well as safety, health and person. But although in some areas the government's authority is widely respected and citizens have a proper sense of duty, experience in America and abroad seems to indicate that the citizen does not look with favour upon the legislation of morals by the government. It is regarded as an inappropriate governmental function; it violates civil rights, the right to privacy and generally the right to hold differing opinions. For example, legislation of this kind may lead to censorship or even the burning of books.

Accordingly, if, unlike socialist-communist regimes, the main responsibility for enforcing morals is not to be the political state, the burden falls back on the church and the family. The school system in America has some difficulty coping with this area because religious doctrine, per se, may not be taught in courses dealing with that subject in government-financed schools, but instead must be approached obliquely through history, civics and other secular courses.

In effect, therefore, most of the responsibility winds up with religion and philosophy because parental responsibilities in this area have also become greatly relaxed, except amongst traditionalist churchgoers who, in terms of membership statistics, are still a majority, but in terms of attendance are now a minority of the population.

Who, exactly, is going to develop new norms to deal with new offences and clarify the interpretation of the old commandments? A couple of examples will illustrate the complexity of the problem. The Bible says, 'Thou shalt not kill.' But does this include the losses of human life due to wars and other conflicts? Does it apply to Jews and Arabs? To Protestants and Catholics in Northern Ireland? In addition, a growing number of vegetarians now contend that it is immoral to kill animals for man's use, and one sees bumper stickers reading, 'Do not kill animals, love them.' What does religion have to say to all these queries? The 'safe' thing to do is to avoid discussing them at all.

Another example of the need to re-examine biblical teaching is in the matter of lust. Does it apply to teenagers, to companionate marriages, to 'office' romances? And if Christ's injunction against even thinking of the sex act outside of marriage is to be strictly obeyed, why is sex increasingly flaunted by what appears in pulp magazines, television performances and pornography in its many forms?

Clergymen of all faiths admonish their members to abide by biblical injunctions relative to adultery, divorce and all related matters, but the tide of non-compliance in recent years has been so great that unless there is a sudden cyclical return to more conservative patterns of the past, it seems unlikely that the clergy, unaided, will be able to cope with a problem of this magnitude.

The modern tendency is to treat this and other related problems mentioned in the Bible as primarily sociological ones rather than to label them as moral. The emphasis is then shifted from moralizing or admonishing to trying to find causes and supply motivations to change. This movement, which goes under the name of 'behavioural science', represents an alliance of psychologists, sociologists,

27

anthropologists, political scientists and medical and health researchers, who try to get at root causes by studying human drives.

For example, if other cultures, such as Japan, seem able to handle the sex question with less difficulty because they consider sex as essentially normal and healthy, perhaps this is a remedy others might try. Possibly, the older attitude toward sex is wrong and if we had a different orientation, the excesses and aberrations presently complained of would appear less often. In this, the behavioural scientists find willing allies in those religions that call themselves 'humanist'. Since their concern is with humans and not theology, the natural tendency of the humanists is to concentrate on people in groups rather more than might be true if the orientation were more towards theology. Perhaps, therefore, this source of interest in social and human problems will supply some of the attention to morality which conventional religions find it difficult to handle alone. One reason this may prove true is that ethical culture, fellowship and humanist groups attract intellectuals primarily and these are research-oriented people.

No matter what form the alliance of forces may take during the next few years, or whether the main contribution is secular or church-related, two things seem fairly clear. The first is that problems such as sex, murder, theft and others mentioned in the Bible, require understanding and deep research, even more than preaching from the pulpit. Ministers will need expert assistance from other professions, as doctors and lawyers now do.

Secondly, one of the connotations of morality, namely, duty, needs somehow to be revitalized. We are here using the term 'duty' as the equivalent of the individual's assuming *responsibility* for his acts and their consequences. It is a motivational problem. It is mainly because individuals lack a sense of pride and responsibility that they produce offspring at the age of fifteen, or earlier, or engage in vandalism out of a sense of hostility and meanness.

One other positive suggestion is this. There has been much fine religious thinking and writing that has occurred since the last part of the Bible was written, several decades after the death of Christ. These writings should be more frequently collated and published. They should be encouraged because they focus on the main problems that confront people today. Religion should be considered a growing thing, responding to new needs and problems through new insights and applications of old truths. It is time our theologians were less defensive and timid. No sacred book is threatened simply because the clergy decides to sponsor more recent religious writings. The Bible would be applied to modern problems, its truth and importance not diminished in the least.

Our final suggestion is the need for a positive, incentive, remedial approach to morality if it is to prove adequate to human needs in a complex world. An example of this is the proverb, 'A workman is worthy of his hire.' Religion should have more to say than now about fair shares and the avoidance of exploitation. Or, again, the adage, 'Idle hands are Satan's ally.' Providing work – especially for the young – is as much a religious problem as a political, social and economic one, and yet most churchgoers seem to accept the proposition that technology will indefinitely limit employment opportunities.

Most problems of sex, drugs and juvenile crime are caused by lack of motivation and by an enforced idleness. Moral injunctions are still true, but sometimes they are not relevant because they fail to deal with the structural problems of social life and they make little attempt to focus on the psychological truths that, for aeons of time, have caused drunkards to become teetotalers, wife-beaters to become doting grandfathers, and leather-jacketed young men self-made businessmen.

Duty and virtue are intertwined. Virtue is motivation, a positive joyful attitude toward life. It is not, as some seem to think, a life-long protection of innocence. It is venturing to dare, being fulfilled. Life and morality are both the product of making potential flower into its full bloom.

5 Religion and Ethics

Ethics is part of the operating side of religion in daily life and hence deserves careful and consecutive thought. Hardly a day goes by without some mention in the news media of the need for ethics or the attempt to regulate ethics. Codes of ethics have been adopted by the Congress of the United States and by the British Parliament to deal with conflicts of interest and outright dishonesty in the conduct of public officials in their relations with interest groups. Among the English-speaking countries, Britain has pioneered in this area, Parliament having passed rules concerning post-government employment as early as 1937. The medical associations are agitated as never before about the ethical questions of creating human life in test tubes and fee splitting for work that in some cases is not even done by the physician who profits financially. In America, the lawyers are seeking more effective ways of enforcing higher ethical standards among lawyers and judges. Businessmen are sometimes heard to express doubts as to whether the excesses of competition and capitalism are a contributing factor in people's turning against the market system. In all such instances, there are two main ways in which the problem is being approached, either by passing government legislation to set the standards and avoid the excesses, or secondly, by the profession's exercising its own self-governing authority to enforce these standards without resort to legislation. This whole subject is interestingly developed in the 1971, 1972, 1973 and 1980 volumes of the British journal of *Public Administration*, published by the Royal Institute of Public Administration in London.

In the conflict of competing ideologies, the communists exploit the idea of 'socialist ethics', contending that their moral aims and actions are superior to those of capitalism. They argue that socialism does not suffer from the contradictions of capitalism and hence contend that the probity both capitalism and socialism seek is inherently more likely to emerge under socialist motivations than those of capitalism.

Beginning shortly after the middle of the nineteenth century in England and the United States, when secular solutions began to be thought of as substitutes for religious sanctions, the idea became popular among scholars that ethics – the cement that holds society together – is a force for good in free countries and would have far more chance of succeeding if it were detached from its theological antecedents and were treated thereafter as merely a rigorously intellectual matter. As part of this intellectual movement to de-theologize the field of ethics, many intellectuals turned against idealism and mysticism as well. Nowhere has this idea been stated with greater acerbity than in the article on 'Ethics' in the *Encyclopedia of Social Sciences* of 1937 (Macmillan): once the elements of the ideal are invoked, 'conduct may lose its tang and concreteness by being too much under the aspect of eternity.' To add still further to this challenge to the religious origins of ethics, influential thinkers and writers such as John Watson, John Dewey and B. F. Skinner developed the idea of the relativity of ethics. Ethics, they contended, are not 'absolute' but are 'situational'. The right thing is right under a certain set of circumstances, but it may be inappropriate in dissimilar circumstances.

In the history of religious thought, it has been customary to trace a hierarchical linkage from the idea of God to morals and from morals to ethics, ethics being the concrete application of moral principles. Similarly, in the history of philosophy, ethics was first considered a 'science' and perhaps the most useful concept in community life, only later to be regarded as a calculus of advantage or disadvantage and pleasure and punishment. It is not surprising, therefore, that in the connotations of the term suggested by standard dictionaries, prominence is given to the idea that ethics consists of the rules of conduct recognized in certain professional or custom-sanctioned areas of human life.

Some of the reasons why religion has lost ground to the secular have been suggested in our essay on morals. Mere prohibitions against killing, divorce and other matters, are too negative, and ethics is positive. It is a 'how to' subject. Equally, when the positive values are emphasized, it is sometimes unclear, from the context, how one is to translate meekness into honesty, peace-making into will-power, or respect into avoidance of the temptation to enrich oneself by seizing opportunity.

To be more concrete, if the religious person is to make his ethics a philosophy of life, he must first develop the framework of a philosophy. This means taking theological truths and seeing how they all fit together into a whole. Failing in this, the religious person inevitably becomes confused by a mixture of contradictions and does not receive the respect or satisfaction he otherwise would.

In a society where there is so much freedom, and consequently more room to manoeuver, the temptations to do shady things are bound to occur frequently. A man professing to believe in Christian charity, for example, may claim deductions on his income tax returns for charitable purposes, but may in fact contribute less than he claims. A person can sell armaments, for example, knowing that almost certainly they will be used to kill people, but he rationalizes that if he withheld the sale, some other country would supply the armaments which might be used against the interests of his own nation; the sale of armaments becomes almost a patriotic duty. Or, in the case of subversion, an innocent man's character may be blackened, but if, as a consequence, a dangerous subversive is thereby caught, the action is excused on patriotic grounds.

The complexities of our age put strains on the ruggedness of character a person would like to have, strains which greatly exceed the temptations afforded two hundred, or even a hundred, years ago. The standard dictionaries quite rightly say that in its finest manifestation ethical behaviour takes the form of a person's character. He has the wisdom and strength to forego personal advantage when the opportunity, while possibly not actually illegal, is contrary to his code. The test of character, as of morals or law, is the fitness of the contemplated act. John Dewey was right in saying that when people act in this manner, they are not necessarily being idealists – they also have a strong sense of community and of what religion teaches concerning communal solidarities.

Another difficulty the religious person experiences arises in a quarter where ordinarily one would not expect it to create a problem. The modern tendency for decisions as to ethics is to rely on the mandates of the law. Instead of saying, 'If it is authorized by law it is legal', a person slips into the habit of saying, 'If it is legal it is ethical.' But, unfortunately, this is not always true. The reason is found in an understanding of the way in which law has developed in recent times. The idea seems to be to regulate one area of conduct after another and in each of these areas, lawyers, legislatures, courts and administrators spin out complicated sets of rules which purport to tell individuals what they may or may not do. Quite naturally, therefore, and without giving much thought to the matter, the average individual falls into the habit of thinking that if there is a rule, the conduct is ethical; and if there is not a rule, the proposed action must be unethical or otherwise there would be a rule.

But rules are confusing. There are more of them than one could fully understand, even if one spent all of his time studying them. And when he does take the pains to study them, he frequently cannot understand the strange and complicated terms in which the rules are couched. The result is that instead of thinking about the rightness or wrongness of the proposed action, he usually acts automatically and with little or no attention to whether his overall philosophy has anything to contribute. Moreover, since he assumes that the law is complete and rules cover behaviour, he judges his intelligence by his ability to find ways of getting around the rules, if it is to his advantage to do so, as in making money or saving taxes.

If a person wishes to qualify as a religious ethicist, therefore, the only option he has is to be one of those rugged characters who were so common at the time of the American Revolution and later in the Victorian era, when the code of a gentleman applied social sanctions which were rather demanding. This is to say that honour is one of the strongest inducements to act in an ethical manner. An honourable man or woman has standards which take the form of a code. If, in addition, such a person has certain religious qualities associated with faith and belief, so much the better.

The relation between one's cosmology and its resulting ethics may be arrived at in the following manner:

The universe consists of existence, vitality, relation, time, order, change, causation and quality.

The instruments of improvement are intellect, volition and affections.

There is one world and everything in it is connected and interacting.

The soul has potential.

Creation is essentially beneficent.

Integrated development is the ideal.

Happiness is making others happy.

On the basis of these assumptions, the ethical aspirations which transcend the secular requirements provided by rules consist of the following:

1. Be true to nature. This means being true to one's nature, God's nature and the laws of the universe, which are creativity, balance and growth.

2. Seek to improve. This involves growth, using the potential of the soul. Help others to grow instead of exploiting them.

3. Seek balance. Do not be extreme, as in giving vent to anger and hostility. Seek equanimity and wisdom. Avoid acquisitiveness for possession's sake and resist the thirst for power and domination.

4. Help others. The affections are natural and are the qualitative factor in life. There is no balance worthy of being called selfhood until intellect and emotions are integrated. Avoid self-centredness.

5. Create an élan or an ideal in one's own mind and consciousness. Beauty and symmetry can be attained.

It will be seen that not much attention has been given to the aberrations or opposites of ethical religious ideals, aberrations which are customarily called 'sins'. This is because religion ought to be essentially positive and not negative. We ought to avoid ethical terms which sound excessively puritanical. Otherwise, there is a danger of making religious ethics sound austere and unbalanced and balance is one of the three most vital principles of life.

Henry Fairlie, in his book *The Seven Deadly Sins Today* (University of Notre Dame Press 1978), ascribes the origin of this list to Gregory the Great and the ruminations of monastic orders. Later the idea was incorporated into orthodox Christian belief. Surely, to meet today's more complicated circumstances, the list could be updated and made more complete.

Fairlie calls himself a 'reluctant disbeliever' who would like to believe in God but is intellectually unable to do so. This honesty is a good ethical instinct and his candor is much to be admired. Even more interesting is his explanation of cause-and-effect relationships. All seven sins – pride, envy, anger, sloth, avarice, gluttony and lust, – says Fairlie, are due to the absence of love. Sin is the perversion of the love of which we are all capable. By excess or neglect we erode our capacity for love.

This is a reasonable doctrine. One wishes, however, that he would probe more deeply into a matter such as anger, particularly from a psychological point of view. Anger may be due to surprise, moral indignation, the instinct to flee, or a number of other things. And psychologically, when it is due to an insufficiency of love, the love that may be lacking initially and in sufficient quantity is the love that is called self-respect. All of which illustrates how complex and difficult an analysis of ethics, as values and codes of conduct, really is.

Professional associations should, of course, continue to elevate and apply higher ethical standards, for much may be accomplished this way and there has been altogether too little effort expended in this direction. The ethical codes in America of the American Medical Association, the American Bar Association, or the International City Managers' Association and in Britain, the British Medical Association, are examples of what can be done. When consistently applied and followed up, these grass-roots efforts have produced beneficial results that are measurable. Nevertheless, ethical standards are likely to be both more pervasive and more durable if they originate in and are buttressed by hard, honest, intellectual probing. Also, if they take their origin from a theology or philosophy of religion that is based upon understandable and workable assumptions. In a chapter called 'The Ethical Ideals Underlying the British Philosophy of Administration', Rosamund Thomas, in her book entitled *The British Philosophy of*

Administration (Longman 1978), has indicated how this might be done.

The ethical confusion in the Western world will never be resolved simply by enunciating more rules. The malaise will continue until a closer connection has been re-established between basic religious truths, codes of morals, and self-induced standards of ethics. An understanding of the conditions existing today will indicate what religious people might do to strengthen the bonds between the elements just mentioned.

A materialistic society in which everyone tries for wealth and power creates a condition in which manipulation flourishes. Having little or no respect for government, we have a correspondingly low regard for the law the political state makes and enforces. In the real world of the market place and the city hall, one of the tests of success is the ability to get around the law, if it results in enrichment for a selfish purpose. Manipulation is based upon a low regard for others and for oneself. It is the modern fashion, among intellectuals especially, to equate manipulation with rationality instead of lack of respect for God and his creatures, which was the older view. Power and wealth are associated in the modern mind with superior intelligence. Intelligence is defined as rationality or the absence of emotion and subjective factors, such as a belief in God, which is considered a myth instead of a reality.

One of the consequences of this rationalist-manipulative view of ethics is that social sentiments are slow to develop. A person who spends his life making his pile seems to have few satisfactions because his lifestyle is narrowly self-centred. He is continually grinding a wheel or looking for escape. By contrast, a person with a unified view of religion develops a humanistic life-style. He has a strong sense of responsibility, not only to himself, but to others.

The inevitable consequence of substituting a rationalist for a religious philosophy, is to promote the class state. The steps in the analysis proceed as follows: the self-interested rationalist gets the lion's share of 'values', which are defined as economic goods and political influence; the organized political state is the distributor of these values and therefore it is in a person's interest to try to control the government and the means of influencing public opinion. Whether the

37

objective is to assure worker or business control of the government, each must be able to staff the government and run its internal affairs if the philosophy of self-interest is to be assured of success. Inevitably, therefore, the government becomes elitist because it excludes the majority, whose basic orientation is different.

Carrying the analysis one step further, when one self-interested sovereign state clashes with another self-interested sovereign state, as increasingly they do at many points, such as use of the seas, outer space and scarce resources, there is little room for compromise and accommodation because in both cases the intellectual imperative is national self-interest. This danger is greater, of course, where one government is worker and another is capitalist controlled, but, to a lesser degree, the same inherent clash is inevitable amongst those nations calling themselves socialist-communist or capitalist-democratic. The stronger the feeling of self-interest, the less latitude there is for discovering common areas of agreement.

The religious orientation proceeds quite differently. If there is one world and everything in it was created by God; if there are laws of the universe that require respect for others, sharing and cooperation and the blending of rationality and ideals to achieve universal well-being and balance, in which none have too much and all have enough to remain human; if all beings have potential and no class has a monopoly of ability, then certain conclusions follow.

There is a hierarchy of law which starts with basic beliefs about God and the universe. These can be formulated in terms of moral principles and from them is derived guidance as to the appropriate ethical thing to do when in doubt. It is a rational thing, but in this case it is combined with an equal element of feeling, defined as emotion or moral sentiment. It is not manipulative, for, instead, it stresses human relations. It assumes that gain is ethically reciprocal and not exclusive. As organizations tend to become more complex, the more difficult is consistent ethical behaviour. But if one pays sufficient heed to the interconnections between theology, morals and ethics, the problem is not too complicated for any individual. The main thing to keep in mind is that we all live on God's world by sufferance and if we do not behave ourselves, our progeny, class and kind, are pretty sure to disappear. This realization has a certain humbling effect.

When T. V. Smith, the University of Chicago philosopher, wrote his essay on 'Ethics' in the 1937 *Encyclopedia of the Social Sciences* (Macmillan), he was as sure as anyone could be that the era of religiously-inspired ethics was over and that secular standards and responsibilities would have to fill in the void. Thirty-odd years later, the heralded demise of religious responsibility in this area seems somewhat premature. If each of us would think more frequently through his cosmology and at the same time resolve to avoid manipulation, hypocrisy and complacency, the religious revival, which most commentators now recognize, might in time clarify a complex topic in a manner never before equalled.

6 The Law and the Prophets

Not all prophets in world history have been mad, although most people at the time assumed them to be. There have always been a few, of course, who merely wanted to call attention to themselves, but their artifice was soon discovered by their contemporaries. As for the sincere, people often accused the prophet who was religiously inspired of being addled because he insisted on the people's religious thought becoming relevant, when their disposition, as ever, was to be complacent. The people, and especially the oligarchy, wanted law and rules, not analysis of evil and impending change.

The number of legitimate prophets in world history is nowhere near so great as is commonly supposed; it is only that what they lacked in numbers was more than offset in influence. We remember them today, many of them, like Isaiah, even when we forget their contemporaries who were better known at the time.

Prophecy is a 'gift'. If it succeeds in combining the best of heart and mind, in a message that is relevant to the time and condition and still based upon timeless principles – and some, not all, perform this feat – the prophet may be the most useful citizen of his age. But in retrospect generally, rarely at the time.

Organized religions become restive and concerned when prophets appear suddenly on the horizon. They have an unsettling effect, especially on the rich and influential who are the main financial support of the church. The main charge brought against the critic of people's morals is that he tends to interfere with the complacency that people seek in religion. The generality of people, in any religion, seek peace of mind as perhaps their most important reason for being interested in religion. If they have sinned or have guilty consciences, they expect the minister to give them absolution and this makes them feel better.

The minister usually hopes to do more than this, of course – to correct the fault, breathe a new spirit into the offender – and often he succeeds. But, after a short experience with 'saving souls', the minister learns that, by native disposition, most communicants are primarily interested in 'feeling good', avoiding the nagging they sometimes get at home and experiencing the soothing effect they desire when the minister walks into the drawing room or into the pulpit on Sunday. It is human nature. The businessman has enough troubles during the week without being upset by something the minister says. The farmer is suffering from drought or insect invasions and what he wants is encouragement, not admonitions concerning his or the country's spiritual health.

On a country-wide level, where the greatest prophets have made their lasting reputations for speaking out against the iniquities of institutions, the considerations are much the same. Businessmen feel prickly when the minister dares to speak about the ethics of business. His business constituent feels – and often rightly – that he knows more about business than the would-be prophet does and therefore he wants to be left alone. In politics, which is even more controversial and more often in the public mind, public policy is looked upon as the domain of the expert. Everyone knows that politics is concerned with power and privilege and consequently those who profit from the *status quo* feel more secure when gentlemen of the cloth leave this area alone. Again human nature comes into play. It is more comfortable to live in two worlds, the world of the practical and the world of the ideal. The minister is regarded more highly if he confines himself to the latter and if he has little to say about the world of power and intrigue. Any reference to 'politics' is thought to be outside the purview of the church and hence had better be avoided.

Against this case for complacency and treading softly, there is, both analytically and historically, a strong argument to be made for the prophetic role in religion. In the progress of human affairs, there is often a plateau which causes individuals and nations to attempt stubbornly to maintain the *status quo*, when to do so is like trying to preserve the stillness before the storm. To fail to recognize these periods of near stagnation is as harmful to conservatives as to those who are less satisfied. Further, no individual, however high his principles may be, is ever totally right. In his complacency, he tends to lose the ability to see the mote in his own eyes while acutely detecting it in others! There are dangers in smugness as well as in permissiveness. The more convinced the smug become concerning their own righteousness, the easier it is to reject the pricks of conscience which affected them more acutely during a prior period, in which they were struggling to improve. All too often, what appears to them to be an admirable 'balance', on closer scrutiny turns out to be a tendency to veer in a direction where, because of lust, cupidity, creature comfort, slothfulness, or hardness of heart, their self-image is either distorted or hypocritical. It is the role of the religious prophet to speak out against these tendencies.

The case for the courageous prophet is even stronger on a national or international scale. The church stands above all other institutions as critic and judge. The church's business is ethics and morals. Without leaders who see, the people perish. The church may not profit from criticizing, but if it fails to speak out when conscience requires it, the church would soon lose its role in the natural scheme of things and at last become little more than a social club. It is almost universally agreed among historians, political scientists, social psychologists and sociologists that by the very nature of institutions – their anonymity and remoteness – one cannot expect as high a standard of morals in government and commerce as that of the individual who has no responsibility except to monitor his own moral behaviour. Although the individual is adept at rationalizations, the political state and the economic power aggregate are naturally so much more adept that there is no comparison in relative magnitudes. We do not, really, hate the citizens of any enemy country, for example, but we hate the things the enemy country stands for; killing is therefore nothing but a necessary incident to what morality requires us to do. Or, again, we do not want Indian peasants to starve, but if the Indian nation will not accede to what is in the United States' vital interest, we will not send them our wheat. Dozens of such examples might be given.

Viewed historically, therefore, it is not at all surprising that the most venerable religious leaders have been prophets as well as teachers

43

of the divine will. Nearly the whole of the Old Testament is the story of great prophets. Almost in the same breath, Isaiah tells his fellow countrymen how to hear God's voice and what they must do to improve their morals if their cities are not to be sacked and burned. And it has been this way down through the records of church history to this day. Jesus said he came not to change the religious law and cause it to fall into disrespect, but he did make it clear that a narrow legalism was not the Lord's will. He believed in the laws of the universe and taught his followers concerning them, but he said that if men and women did not become as little children they would never see the kingdom of heaven. He said the meek would inherit the earth and that the rich man would find it difficult to enter into heaven. He said that the peacemaker would sit at the right hand of God and yet, before this time and during most of the period since his teaching, war has been the scourge of civilization and, more often than not, has been fought over religious differences. We can disregard and have disregarded these inconsistencies, but, if we are able to read, there can be no doubt that Jesus was not only a prophet but a radical one at that.

The prophetic function is out of style nowadays. At the end of the Victorian period, it was considered good form to talk unaffectedly about virtue, wisdom, or even goodness. Today, it is thought naive, sentimental, poor form, not at all scientific. A general scepticism pervades the air. 'Emotional' is a bad word. People even wince when someone uses the word 'truth'. Love is something that happens in the movies or on the television screen. In both Britain and the United States, fifty or a hundred years ago, many prophetic voices were to be heard; today, prophecy is relatively rare. One thinks, for example, of John Wesley and Methodism in religion, John Hobson and H. G. Wells in politics. In the United States, one's mind turns to Walter Raushenbush, Benjamin Kidd, and in politics to William Jennings Bryan, the silver-tongued orator, who became a presidential candidate more than once. Today, the changed mood causes serious scholars to organize societies using the term 'futurism'.

But the virtual stilling of the prophetic voice in recent years does not mean that the breed will never reappear. It will, and soon. America is still recovering from the trauma of anti-communist McCarthyism

44

and the street violence of the 1960s. Underneath the veneer of sophistication which causes intellectuals to reject any show of emotion, there is still, in the American people as a whole, a yearning to return to simple virtues. And, through the ages, that is what prophecy has chiefly relied upon for its appeal.

A prophet is a person who is clairvoyant concerning the future. He is not a prophet simply because he thinks he knows; he must be proved right. The number of persons who are clairvoyant in this pragmatic sense is limited indeed. To begin with, there are in any generation, even among statesmen, very few individuals who have sufficient 'feel' for history to attract much notice and then to demonstrate the ability to project trends in relation to the big cyclical changes that occur in society.

A person does not, however, acquire this clairvoyance simply by immersing himself in history. The reason there are so few prophets is found somewhere else. It is in this matter of 'consciousness', to which reference has several times been made. The true prophet is intuitive, sensitized, part of the unity of life, which transmits signals by something resembling extrasensory perception. If a person has this sensitivity and is part of the conduit system, he becomes a transmitting station in several sectors: in one-to-one relations; in interpersonal relationships; in relation to God. Eventually, this faculty may extend even to inter-planetary communications. True prophets develop these abilities because they seek truth, they search for reality and their systems become attuned to something outside themselves.

But here an important proviso arises: the legitimate prophet must be truthful, purely motivated, the opposite of the charlatan, who is a dissembler. When the Bible refers to people who speak tongues, as it does in discussing the various skills needed to promote the Christian faith, one thinks what Paul must have had in mind was this extrasensory ability. It seems to be intimately related to the soul. Emerson believed this and so do we. Hence our contention that the prophet is the one who has the biggest soul and that the soul comes from attunement with vital forces.

Most great prophets that we revere today have been essentially moralists instead of theologians. The theologian's stance is usually defensive, the prophet's denunciatory, or at least activist. And because this is so, the prophet is exposed to the danger of thinking that 'his' views should prevail. Some, who have been willing to kill whole populations, were clearly not as tolerant nor so loving as the creator himself. Everyone who aspires to be a prophet, therefore, should guard against the ever present danger of becoming a zealot. Anyone who deludes himself into thinking he is *always* right is as dangerous as a deranged animal. Only the prophet who has love in his heart deserves to be respected.

It may now be seen why almost invariably in literature the word 'law' is associated with the role of the prophet. This law is not man-made or even ecclesiastical; it is the law of the universe made by God himself. But, by easy extension, it is perhaps understandable why two quite different connotations often become attached to the root meaning. The first we have identified: the prophet's *own* set of rules, which may or may not be true. The second connotation relates to protocol, ritualistic or traditional taboos, which may or may not be essential to the original meaning of the term 'law'. It is for these sectarian conventions that some religious teachers have fought more fiercely than for the spiritual ties that bind man and God and men in groups together. Amongst theologians, it almost seems, at times, that the more picayune the point, the harder they will argue with each other. It was recognition of this fact that caused Jesus to deal so harshly with the Pharisees – the people who were more interested in form than in substance, in ritual more than in spirit. And yet, as every sociologist knows, this spinning of rituals by the 'in-group' is found in every civilization. It sets them aside from other groups, enhances common loyalties and makes the group feel superior to others.

This connotation of the word 'law' is obviously foreign to the instincts of the true prophet. Morals are more than manners. Etiquette is desirable in its place, but, compared to spirit, it is cosmetic. Formalism of any kind contributes to complacency and to worshipping the artificial instead of the spirit. As the veneer of formalism divides the people, it becomes the enemy of 'consciousness' as we have defined it and the prophet, with his temperament and his chosen mission in life, cannot afford to be held back by it.

The historical reason why law and prophecy have been so often combined in the same phrase is that law, when so used, means God's universal laws of the universe, nothing less. A characteristic of a true prophet is that he holds his allegiance directly to God and no one else. For the sake of the larger vision of reality, the true prophet is willing to suffer the fate of the martyr: stoned, imprisoned, decapitated, forced to drink hemlock. Like Socrates, he is willing to die. But he does not contend that his views must necessarily be forced upon others.

In short, the prophet is quite a rugged character. He may upset some people, especially the complacent and the powerful, but he does it in a selfless and not an egotistical manner. He realizes that it is human nature to substitute the lesser for the greater. He knows that his role is two-pronged: to persuade people to look back to the fount of truth and at the same time look forward to the transitions in society that enable all individuals to climb to greater heights.

A new breed of religious prophet is about to appear. Under the influence of ecology, the people of the world are being psychically conditioned to recognize and act upon the principle of balance, which is all that prevents competing ideologies from destroying a large portion of the earth's population. Some countries, such as China, do not need to learn the philosophy of balance, because they have been practising it for centuries. It was the main element in Confucianism. It is the reason the Chinese have lasted so long and now constitute almost a fourth of the world's population. Western nations, and especially the United States, have been slower to learn the essential truths concerning balance and survival. Now, however, within the past twenty years, the idea of ecology has captured the souls of the West to a far greater extent than our politicians, who are often the last to catch on, seem to appreciate. Ecology has a special appeal to the younger generation – the brats of the 1960s – who first veered toward existentialism to rediscover nature and are now turning back towards organized religion, in a way that will greatly change the church as an institution during the coming century.

There will be more preachers who are prophets. Instead of studying theology as much as ministers have in the past, the new clergy will concentrate on areas that are directly relevant to unsatisfied needs. Such areas of specialization are science, medicine, psychology, aesthetics, conflict resolution and the philosophy of law and economics. After being trained in one of these substantive fields, the new breed of minister will assay the teacher's role, as Jesus did, and will speak out fearlessly as a prophet. Moreover, the new generation will listen to and support the modern prophet, instead of trying to force him to adopt a more conservative mien.

The cosmic reasons why this prophecy is 'safe' rather than 'way-out' is that the differences between the East and West are not nearly so unbridgeable as extremists on both sides seem to think. The communists of all descriptions need Western management know-how and additions to their own limited materialistic philosophies. Similarly, if morale is to be improved and unity restored, the Western nations now recognize that they need to give more attention to a unifying sense of community and unselfish service. Both sides are too material-istic. The Muscovite needs more personal freedom and the amenities that state enterprise is ill-equipped to provide. The American needs a bit more planning and assurance that there will be work for everyone. In such situations, the sensible solution is frequently a matter of learning from each other.

Whether this *rapprochement* will occur after a third world war has greatly reduced the earth's population, or whether its coming will be the reason such a holocaust has been avoided, is unclear. Both sides have been proceeding on the basis of a false psychological assumption since the Cold War started in 1946. The balance of terror does not guarantee peace. Nations armed to the teeth need only an 'accident', such as a button touched at the wrong time, or a national insult that was not intended, to loose the irrational lusts and angers that are incapable of calculating risks, much less benefits and losses.

There will be no peace until war is renounced. War will not be renounced until East and West decide that they are not so very differ-ent. These insights are not likely to come from governments, but from outside of government. That is the challenge of the religious prophet of the waning years of the twentieth century.

7 Sin

In one way or another religion and concern about sin have always been related. It is said that Calvin Coolidge, the American President, attended church alone one Sunday. On returning home Mrs Coolidge asked what the sermon was about. He answered, 'Sin'. She queried further, 'What did he say about it?' She received the laconic answer, 'He was agin it.' The church has been aligned consistently against sin and this may be one of the reasons why it has not been more successful. Not that the church should be in favour of sin, but rather that it might have a more discriminating approach to the problems of human behaviour. Traditionally, the interest of the church and its clergy has been largely either redemptive or manipulative. The possibility of a third position has emerged with contemporary research into the nature of the human being. It is this third alternative that we would explore. Biblical insight seems to warrant the exploration of this third alternative.

The last few decades have witnessed considerable discussion of the forms of behaviour we have traditionally called sinful. Freudian interest in eliminating life-impairing restraint on healthful behaviour has been interpreted as a destruction of moral standards and the invitation to licentious action. This misinterpretation was followed by a movement in the other direction by those who followed the lead of O. Hobart Mowrer, the psychiatrist and professor who discovered sin as a valid tool in psychotherapeutic intervention, with the effort to reinstitute sin and the responsibility that went with managing it as a necessity for maturity. Karl Menninger lifted the discussion to a more comprehensive focus with his books on *The Crime of Punishment* (Viking 1966) and *Whatever Became of Sin?* (Hodder

1975). Within the church, we can no longer act as if this new perspective on sin did not exist. In fact, we may find that the new focus comes closer to the New Testament ideal than we have been willing to believe.

We have been inclined to think that sin is essentially a body problem. The dualism implicit in this approach to sin assumes that the body and its appetites are constantly compromising the purity of the spirit. In this battle, when the body wins it is sin and when it loses we are safe. But the basic monism of our day sees the cause-effect relationships as basic to life and inevitably producing unity of being. The research in psychosomatic medicine tends to affirm this unity.

Perhaps we understand the functional dichotomy that appears to produce the dualism when we trace human responses to the birth of consciousness. Before there was self-consciousness, or social-consciousness, there was no possibility of morality or ethical dilemmas. Instinct reigned. It was neither good nor bad. Primitive persons were amoral. They were incapable of sin. Then the Bible records the distress that came with the emergence of consciousness and the capacity for sin. Adam and Eve personified this emergence. They developed a capacity for discriminating action and violated it. They did what they knew they should not do. They felt guilt. They tried to escape from blame. They felt subject to punishment. The burden of consciousness rested heavily on them. They could not retreat to a former state of paradise where they were oblivious of moral consequences. They were aware of a cosmic dimension of their behaviour for they violated God's will, or so they interpreted their feelings. When the next generation felt the weight of this burden of consciousness, they were aware of its social meaning and Cain tried to deny and escape from his obligation to respect others.

So we see that the idea of personal sin was born with the idea of self-consciousness and the idea of social obligation was developed with the awareness of obligation to others. In its earliest representation, we see self-consciousness leading to the idea of sin, social-consciousness leading to the idea of responsibility and cosmic-consciousness making possible the whole idea of temptation, self-mastery that leads to spiritual growth, or self-indulgence that is characterized as sin.

It is this conflict that we see developed in another form in the New Testament. Paul speaks clearly of one aspect of the problem of sin when he says, 'The wages of sin are death.' His emphasis echoes the Old Testament idea of punishment and the violation of God's will as the basis for various forms of punitive action. It was even questioned whether compassion for the ill was not an interference with God's retribution. Jesus, on the other hand, symbolized the compassion that would heal, redeem and redirect life. His emphasis was on the grace that could restore the goals for worthy living. This ontological emphasis was in contrast to Paul's emphasis on the burden of the past with its inescapable consequences. For Jesus, the resolution of the problem of sin through self-mastery was the basis for eternal life.

It may well be that the two emphases may be brought into a valid working relationship. It is at this point that the wise and discriminating emphasis of the New Testament teaching of Jesus may help us resolve the problem. Sin is not monolithic. It is a composite of at least three ingredients. There is overt behaviour that can be evaluated, there is a group climate and social pressure that determines the acceptability of the behaviour and there is its motivation.

Overt behaviour that is equated with the sinful is usually clearly self-destructive, or an act against other persons and the extensions of the persons in the rights of property and personal freedom of action. We hear the phrase 'victimless crimes'. Probably there are no forms of criminal behaviour that do not adversely affect the lives of some persons, but this is where legal definitions tend to modify the assessment of behaviour.

Motivation raises other issues. For well over a hundred years in courts of law the M'Naughton Rule has been employed to evaluate the motivation for acts that would otherwise be considered unlawful. This practice of considering motives is applied to the behaviour of children, the aged and the ill. If the person whose behaviour is in question is not capable of adequate self-evaluation, then the sinful burden is reduced or nullified completely. So temporary insanity is often the form of legal escape from the burden of personal responsibility for antisocial behaviour. If a person is not able to control his behaviour because of motivational breakdown, then the effects must be assessed in the light of that breakdown. So, clearly, the matter of motivation is important in the cause-effect process that is necessary for determining the nature of sin.

Third is the matter of social acceptance or pressure. We know well that what is sinful in one context is considered to be heroic behaviour in another. Murder is a sin against a person, unless it has the social sanction of war. Even murder in self-defence is subject to reduced culpability. When one of us was screening Greek citizens for marriage to American personnel, he was interested to find that prostitution by a poor girl to build up her dowry was not only acceptable but an admired form of dedication to her future home. What our State Department thought of as 'moral turpitude' or depravity, in another culture had the marks of nobility. So behaviour and its motivation are always subject to the accepted moral standards of a given society. What is sin in one place or time may not be so in other circumstances.

These distinctions have been confirmed and elaborated in contemporary personality studies. The terminology may be different, but the impact of its assessment of sinful behaviour is not incompatible with deeply rooted practice in human history. Sub-rational behaviour may be rooted in the independent function of the primitive brain, the diencephalon, which controls the function of hunger, thirst, sex and self-defence. Under stress or acute pain, the primitive brain can separate itself from the cortical or judgmental regions of the brain and function independently. It has been reported that starving prisoners in a concentration camp may become 'like animals' in their struggle for bits of food. Sub-rational behaviour in relation to the strong sex drive is often observed and much violent behaviour is in the context of intimate relations. When people feel threatened, they may 'go berserk', which is another way of saying that sub-rational drives take over the behaviour. Much that is equated with sinful behaviour is related to these powerful, but uncontrolled, drives operating within the nervous system of a person.

Non-rational behaviour is also a factor. In the developmental emergence of the personality, there may be influences that cause permanent damage to the capacity for meaningful relationships. For instance, the sociopath may have no capacity for feeling with others, something basic to normal human relationships. The sociopath uses and manipulates people for selfish purposes. The cause of this damaged personality seems to be rooted in early life when the capacity for trust and relationship was developed. If this growth process was fractured, or thwarted, the person may be as crippled in personality as a thalidamide victim is deformed in body. Most criminals appear to be sociopathic. Many young blacks coming out of sadly deprived backgrounds seem to fall into this category. Their behaviour is the result of social deprivation and the motivational problems cannot be easily separated from the inadequacies operative in mis-shaping their personalities.

In addition to sub-rational and non-rational forms of behaviour, there is also the social consciousness or group awareness that is basic to the assessment of meaning of behaviour. In the religious context, a lack of awareness of responsibility is called sin and, in the legal structure, the same behaviour may be called crime. The mentally ill, or personality deprived, have truncated capacity for social awareness. Modern modes of thought concerning personality and responsibility take into account also the capacity for social awareness in determining what is sinful or criminal.

These recent developments in relation to understanding the motivation for behaviour give us a new perspective for looking at the history of religion as it has dealt with sin. There seem to have been three major emphases, even though no one emphasis has been entirely exclusive of some of the elements of the others in practice. First was the manipulative approach to sin. This has often been used by established institutions and evangelists. The manipulative approach used the assumption of sin as a device to gain control over people. First there was the effort to make people aware of their sinfulness, then offer them a simplistic approach to resolving their sin and then stimulate the action that could put the simplistic formula in motion. Usually this took the form of a hellfire and brimstone sermon to frighten the hearers, then offer indulgences for sale, or a love offering, or a promise of salvation by holding up a hand or walking towards an altar. Then there was the effort to bind the person to a programme of action that would extend control into the future. This kind of approach was without discrimination of individual needs and was applied in a manner that rode roughshod over human sensibilities. Often it was more sinful in its total impact than the behaviour that it railed against, and seemed incompatible with the New Testament concern for people and their inner spiritual development. Yet it still seems to be the most prevalent approach to sin in terms of organized religion.

A second approach has been to create a self-concept that was consistently damaging. This was the effort to perceive self as sinful, helpless to cope and 'like a worm' in the sight of God. Here a theological emphasis on a divine substitutionary atonement took responsibility for life out of the hands of the individual, who was helpless, and put it in the hand of God, who was all-powerful. This reduced human self-esteem, created endless guilt and remorse and violated the basic teaching of the New Testament about the value of human life and the need for growth in responsibility and self-esteem. While this creation of impotence on the part of the individual was damaging, its main impact was to destroy the personal obligation and relationship the individual had with God. It impaired the partnership between God and the human being and replaced it with a servitude that destroyed the internal resources for managing sin. It also tended to create a non-discriminatory approach to human behaviour, that made it easy to use subtle manipulation in the place of crude and irresponsible abuse of neurotic guilt.

A third approach has been more sensitive to the emphasis of the New Testament on understanding, compassion and stimulus to growth and personal adequacy. Here the effort has been to encourage and inspire people to assume responsibility for their own lives. In the place of vengeance on God's part and the punitive approach so often found in the Old Testament, there was an emphasis on love, a discovery of a new and more life-fulfilling direction and the use of the abundant resources of God to build a more abundant life. This approach allowed for a more discriminating view of sin and emphasized a re-education for life.

Where there was sub-rational behaviour, with all of its powerful life-drives, there was an effort to create the forms of self-understanding that could build inner resources, rather than the self-condemnation that reduced any capacity for constructive self-understanding and self-control. At this point, the Sermon on the Mount seems to be the highest expression of this need not to deny the existence of the basic life-drives, but rather to use them for inner growth. In this powerful statement, Jesus gives the formula for spiritualizing basic life-energy. Lust then can become love, hunger and thirst can be turned into a quest for righteousness, and even death, the ultimate form of insecurity, can be turned into a source of inner strength and mourning can bring fortitude and the skill of coping.

Where there was non-rational behaviour, there could develop modes of therapeutic intervention. As with the Gaderene demoniac, instead of the restraint of ropes and chains, the isolation from the normal community bonds, the effort to restore humanity and normal communication has its beneficial effects. Therapeutic intervention may well be part of the redemptive process. The healing power of forgiveness of self, others and of disturbed attitudes toward cosmic reality, may so modify life that the reoriented perspectives can give release from fear and anxiety, guilt and remorse, and let loose in life a newly discovered and more healthful inner being.

Where there is despairing behaviour that reduces life and its meaning, the impulse toward destructive behaviour may emerge for values are affected and nothing seems to make any difference. Here another ingredient may be added to understanding and therapeutic intervention. Inspiration, the in-spiriting of the individual with new motives and better purpose, may move life out of the slough of despond toward creative action. When all three of these elements are combined, the goals of New Testament action against sin may be realized.

Jesus understood that sinful attitudes were disruptive of life and destructive of persons. But he seemed to feel that sin was its own punishment and adding retribution to the suffering that already existed was adding insult to injury. His major interest seemed to be to help people get beyond the life-impairing behaviour to new perspectives and higher motivations. He avoided the kind of judgment that caused further suffering. He called for endless forgiveness – seventy times seven. Instead of open condemnation, he offered a better way and then said, 'Go and sin no more.'

His prescription seemed to be to establish right relations with God for then there would be a high value on life and a value system that was commensurate with this high self-esteem. Then life would tend to invest in that enriched life and there would be no impulse towards self-abasement and the compensations that tried to make a miserable life a bit less miserable. Actually, it seems that sinful behaviour is less apt to plague life when life is so rewarding that a mystic awareness touches all of life with wonder and glory. This is the essence of the Sermon on the Mount. This attitude showed through the behaviour of Jesus. This attitude toward understanding, therapeutic intervention and a more rewarding vision of the possibilities of life, brings the best of the New Testament into accord with the best insights of research in the personality sciences.

The problem of sin is too important to be left to ancient myths and legends and institutional designs for manipulating vulnerable people. It is important to explore the implications of consciousness as they affect behaviour. It is also important to understand the sub-rational and non-rational forces that are at work to influence behaviour. Only then will we be in a position to examine the behaviour we speak of as sinful, objectively. Only then will we be able to see sin for what it is: unhealthy forms of behaviour emerging from developmental abnormalities, social pressures and disturbed consciousness. Then it may be that we will understand that sin itself is a myth developed to gain and maintain control over people by a priestly class who found this was the easiest way to gain control and exert power.

The loving, compassionate approach to the human dilemma that is revealed in the teachings of Jesus gives us warrant to look again at human behaviour to see what it tells us about the struggle to find the good life in the presence of primitive drives and developmental defects in personality. Only then will we be in a position to take the discriminating approach to behaviour that makes it possible for us to know when understanding is needed, when therapy is needed and when people need to be inspired to discover their own resources for achieving a more abundant use of the resources God makes available for the good life. We have too long punished, burdened with guilt and assaulted consciousness with a concept of sin that came from an imperceptive past. The future calls for more than myths and crimes of punishment. It calls rather for a creative relationship of the inner being with the cosmic being, that can enrich life and make healthful behaviour the desirable alternative to self-destruction. Then, and only then, it seems that the promise of Christ's revelation can be made available to mankind and healing, redeeming grace takes the place of fear, futility and fostered failure.

8 Salvation

Almost invariably when we hear of sin, we also hear of means of salvation. Salvation is usually spoken of in non-specific terms, as if some mysterious process were being mediated that makes it possible for sinners to become non-sinners by some quick and easy method that is entrusted to institutions or specialists who are experts in managing the matters related to sin, suffering and salvation.

In our efforts to look objectively at religion and its relevance for life, we cannot escape the responsibility for looking closely at the assumptions and processes that are involved in salvation as it is usually construed. If sin is a religious myth created to guarantee manipulative control over people by institutional religion and its practitioners, the implications of this for our approach to salvation become immediately applicable. If sin is a manipulative concept designed to control people for priestly power, is salvation also a myth that serves a similar and just as unworthy a purpose? Questions such as these immediately invite us to approach our subject from a different perspective.

If what we have traditionally called sin is viewed by the personality sciences as a composite of behaviour, motivation and social standards of judgment, then it logically follows that the methods for managing this composite would have to be looked at in terms of the meaning of the behaviour, motivation and social patterns that are thought of as essential to salvation. We then have to start asking another series of questions if we are to develop an understanding of this traditional concept. Who has power to mediate salvation? Where did the power come from? Is it adaptable or firmly structured? What are people saved from? What are they saved for? Who decides what value system is basic to a system that seeks to mediate salvation and saving grace? Such questions quickly change our focus from revelation to relevance. Such questions move us beyond the queries usually aimed at candidates for salvation such as: 'Do you want to be saved?', 'Will you accept our plan of salvation?', 'Will you deny yourself, take up a cross, and cheerfully and uncritically accept a new life style?', 'In return for the benefits of salvation, will you make the mediating person or institution the beneficiary of your loyalty and at least a share of your possessions?', 'Will you accept the idea that salvation is an event like being born rather than like a process of education, discipline and growth?' Such questions appear to encourage a bargaining approach to a cosmic process which trades personal responsibility for easy magic and personal integrity for a mess of pottage, to use the Old Testament term. The concept of salvation as usually employed by the church and its representatives may tend to become a gimmick to support a power trip that strips persons of their most valued endowment, the right to discover and achieve their own personal fulfilment, their more abundant life, their achievement of an inner kingdom where the human being and the divine being enter into a free and enriching relationship. Then the divine potential in each person becomes the divine actual. In this unique process, it becomes important to find a facilitator rather than a manipulator, one who respects the inner being and its capacity to develop and does not force an abandonment of personal integrity as the prerequisite for salvation.

At this point, then, it becomes important for us to understand what Jesus said and did. It is important to see why his approach was summarily rejected and why a substitute plan of salvation was adopted which is still largely maintained by the persons and institutions that claim the mantle of Christendom.

A confusion about the nature and person of Jesus set in early in Christian history. Paul, who had never met Jesus, put him in a place of cosmic power as Lord of All. Matthew connected Jesus with Jewish history and prophecy. Mark reported Jesus' humanity as current events. Luke developed the Greek perspective with all that implies. John developed a spiritual perspective. In Hebrews, we have developed the Jesus of faith and, in Revelation, the symbolic nature is emphasized so much that the concepts of other parts of the New Testament are obliterated. From this confusion have come differing ideas of the role of Jesus in the plan of salvation. And the one Jesus proclaimed has usually been overlooked.

Tradition has manufactured its own theories of salvation. For instance, in talking with the dean of a Bible School, we were informed that there were seven steps to salvation and, with a sense of unquestioned authority, he listed them as belief in the divine substitutionary theory of atonement, the virgin birth, the physical resurrection, the divine inspiration of every word of scripture, the Apostles Creed, the second birth and the rejection of the theories of evolution. Quite obviously recent history has had an influence on this plan of salvation. Also, it requires that one's brains be parked in order to become eligible.

Other historical efforts to create manipulative theories for achieving 'salvation' include the ransom theory where one special person was given as a ransom for everyone else. This theory tends to absolve mankind from responsibility for life and was tied in with the concept of coming again to save the world. When this did not happen on schedule, the theory was replaced in later times by the satisfaction theory. Here the idea was expressed that sin offends God and the offence is wiped out by the sacrificial death of Christ, which provides God with an acceptable form of recompense for his cosmic suffering. This theory was based on a concept of a small-sized God, easily offended and capricious in nature, whose petulance could be manipulated by a crude deal. As perspectives on the universe expanded, a new theory emerged which was built around the effects of contemplating the Cross. Here the theory was that as men confronted the sufferings of Christ on the Cross, they would be ashamed, filled with remorse and so would abandon their sinful ways. None of these theories seemed to have a very exalted idea of God and their staying power historically was limited by their inadequacy.

The traditional theories of salvation either emphasized a scapegoat theory of God or a pascal lamb theory of Jesus. They did not have a New Testament concept of either the nature of man or of God. Contemporary theories of salvation seem to do little better. Four such theories are in current vogue. We will look briefly at these.

First is the approach generally followed by those who have a funda-mentalist orientation. They usually require as a starting point an unquestioning attitude toward the scriptures. So it becomes easy to take things out of context and ignore an overall picture as an alterna-tive to a more rational observation of human needs and basic resources for meeting those needs. It emphasizes the substitution of divine resources for human effort or responsibility. The theme is self-abandonment and the affirmation 'that Jesus does it all'. When persons have made a mess of life and are at the end of their resources, they are in the psychological state that can easily give up on responsibility and wise self-management and can throw it all over on the shoulders of a cosmic entity who will never fail. It is the approach of the hymn that sings, 'What a friend we have in Jesus, all our sins and griefs to bear.' Assuming that there might be such a patient and long suf-fering being, what does it do to the person who is able to jettison all of life's responsibilities and burdens by putting them on another? If a person would not treat an earthly friend in such an unreasonable manner, what warrant is there for subjecting a cosmic friend to such indignity? This essentially escapist approach to life makes God into an easily manipulated scapegoat and encourages the person to retreat further from reality into the unlikely state of being recreated in a second process of birth. This popular form of escape from maturity and life-responsibility seems to have its appeal in a magical process of retreating to a dependency relationship just at the point in life where independence of attitude and action is basic to mature living and wise life-management. It seems to be the exact opposite from the stern discipline that would accept responsibility for the creating of an inner kingdom where the spirit of God would feel at home.

Second is a simplistic plan of salvation that is well adapted to the manipulative approach. This is most familiar in the activities of mass media evangelists and illustrated well by the approach of Billy Graham. The setting is almost always the same – the symbols of success in large crowds, the creating of an atmosphere of showmanship with music, staging and spectacular people and dramatic episodes. Then in that setting a three step programme is almost invariably followed. A sermon is employed to make people aware of their plight and stimu-late the strong emotions that come with neurotic guilt. This form of guilt, deeply rooted in the developmental processes of the personality, appears to be almost universal, the exceptions being the sociopath or the psychopath who seem to lack a capacity for this type of feeling. So an assault on neurotic guilt is bound to have a profound impact on the emotions of many people. When the feelings of guilt have been activated, the second step is to present a simplistic solution so that the human problems are minimized and the simplistic solution is made to look inviting. The third step is to invite a simple response that can separate the person from the problems and the guilt. This may be as simple as lifting a hand, walking to the front of the auditorium or promising to become a tither for life. In the atmosphere of emotional support and group enthusiasm, the response to a simplistic programme such as this may be numerically large, but relatively small in terms of its impact on life. With an eloquent speaker, a promise of salvation and a simple act or two with the assurance of low commitment and large gain, it is almost a sure thing for the statistics of the evangelist, even though there is little residue in the lives of the people who have engaged in a little game-playing but not much more. Most people who play the game have the feeling that there is everything to gain and nothing to lose, so why not? But this type of game-playing plays fast and loose with the sacred precincts of personality and employs a cynical form of manipulation that is more attuned to the unconscionable attitude of the sociopath than it is the deep reverence and respect for human personality and the promise of a more abundant life for the disciplined kingdom that Jesus talks about.

A third approach to salvation in contemporary religious activity is the trivialization that is demonstrated in the writing and preaching of Norman Vincent Peale. Here we find a mixture of low demands on life, large promises for success and happiness, served up with a series of formulas that have little or no relationship to anything that is found in the teaching of Jesus.

The message of Dr Peale and the success he has achieved seem to be related to the needs of obsessive-compulsive neurotics for emotional shoring up on a regular basis. So they get their weekly shot in the psyche and are able to contend with life for a few days until another shot is administered. The motto seems to be, 'Look at the world through rose-coloured glasses and it will smile back at you.' There seems to be little here that speaks to the deep and searing problems of suffering people and a society that is in the throes of self-destructiveness. The inspiring poems and vignettes of successful businessmen who owe it all to a trivial formula say little to the major moral dilemmas of our age or to the anguish of those whose spiritual needs are too deep for a snack of pabulum. Yet it is a distressing commentary on our age that such a message seems to have so great an appeal.

Fourth in the forms of salvation that are preached in our day is the modern interpretation of the message of Paul. Growing out of the experience of guilt and failure in his own life, Paul assumed a stance of self-rejection and punitive action against the self. In the place of the self-assurance that could build on the unique strength of every individual, Paul emphasizes his weakness. His mind, spirit and life-style are supplanted by the mind and spirit and way of the Christ who is the source of the grace that makes it possible for him to function at all. In effect, Paul seeks what in psychological terms might be referred to as a personality transplant. His personal history and endowment are subjected to the personality of another. In this way, he gets beyond his inner conflicts and his deep guilt and becomes a new person in Christ. With the great endowment of his mind and his eloquence and literary style, he has been able to impress upon the history of Christendom this mood of self-denegration with its invitation to escape from personal responsibility by becoming in effect another person. But if we accept the uniqueness of the gift of God in life, we cannot retreat from the obligation to develop life to its most abundant form so that the image of God is not lost in xeroxed copies of another and separate being.

Historically, it seems that the insight of the gospels has been seen darkly through the lens that Paul ground out of his own experience, rather than the inverse where Paul's experience could have been tinctured with the awareness of human potential and human need that was implicit in the teachings of Jesus. The message of Paul was geared to the manipulative ideas of sin and salvation that could be adopted by an institution to serve its own purposes. It reduced the possibilities for developing the inner kingdom and its responsibility for growth toward oneness with God, the source of its life and strength.

In these four contemporary approaches to salvation we see the abandonment of reason because reason is too demanding, the acceptance of manipulation for, as in Germany under Hitler, it was easier to be manipulated than to face stern reality, and with trivialization it was more superficially comforting to be deceived than to face the painful truth. And last, but not least, it was easier to seek a personality transplant than it was to make your own being healthy in its relation to the source of its divine image.

Yet our world is desperately in need of salvation. It needs to be saved from ruthless passions and deep seated perversions of mind and spirit that can easily lead us to destruction. The little and deceptive nostrums have been tried and found wanting. How can we find the resources that can save us from destruction? There seems to be no better way than to rediscover what Jesus was talking about in his own plans for salvation. How can we find it?

Initially, we will have to make a determined effort to rid ourselves of the debris of history. We will have to be willing to sacrifice the institution and its plan for saving itself through the manipulation of its people. We will have to be both courageous and inventive as we seek to discover ways of implementing the message of Jesus as a relevant resource for our world.

Jesus set the goal of an abundant life and the privileges of divine sonship not through mediation but through the forms of revelation that could lead to self-discovery and full self-realization. He had no institution and turned his back on the only institution of his day that might have been considered a possibility, the synagogue. He built his structure in the lives of people, usually those people who were outcast and rejected. He challenged the tradition that had treated women as chattels and second-rate beings to make them spiritual equals. He claimed that children, who were usually regarded as of little importance until they were physically and socially mature, were the great resource for kingdom building and that their role could not be ignored without doing damage to God's kingdom on earth. He saw the diseased not in terms of their illness but rather in terms of their wholeness. He saw the outcast not in terms of their separation but rather in their usefulness as restored members of the community. He saw the religious community not in terms of buildings, traditions and authoritative persons, but rather in terms of the potential for growth into fulfilled persons. He had little place for condemning sinful persons, but rather had a deep concern for what they could become. He opposed self-destroying behaviour in persons and communities, but attacked the behaviour and not the persons. He emphasized the cause-effect processes at work in life and had no truck with magic or miracles. He wanted to help people grow to their full potential.

Jesus made no claims of uniqueness. In fact his emphasis was just the opposite. He praised growth and inner skills. He said that those who accepted his ideas of inner power would be able to do anything he did, but even greater works would occur as they developed their abilities to employ their self-consciousness in active relation to the consciousness of God.

The peddling of cheap salvation seems to be quite the opposite of the mood of Jesus. To sing of 'amazing grace for such a worm as I' is quite out of keeping with the main thrust of the message of Jesus. The quick and easy panaceas for the problems of life seem to have no bearing on the concern of Jesus for accepting personal responsibility for life and developing the inner kingdom until it is a safe haven for inter-relationship between creature and creator.

It may well be that the modern development of the personality sciences, with their greater understanding of personality dynamics and human needs, provides us with some of the perspectives we need in order to read again the words of Jesus and see what they really meant. It may well be that this new insight has come just in time, for our great need for salvation was ill-served by the reductionist emphases of the last two thousand years. It will take adequate people and not self-rejecting, self-reducing persons to face the needs of our day. The plan of salvation that seems to emerge at long last from the newly perceived words of Jesus does not urge a retreat from responsibility, but rather an advance towards it. It does not call for destructive attitudes toward the self, but rather a new appreciation of the privileges and power of self-fulfilment. It invites us to stand up to our full stature as those who can create a better future for ourselves and our world. The history of Christendom has too long fettered the message of Christ. Let us seek to lift the burden of the past and accept the challenge of the future.

We have heard of a man in Alaska who approached a frozen river with trepidation and crawled across it on all fours lest he break through the ice. While he rested on the far shore he saw a large truck loaded with logs coming down the river using it as a highway. Perhaps there is a parable there. Too long have we crawled through history in fright and uncertainty when we could rise to our full stature and know ourselves as those made in the image of God and bequeathed the privileges of divine sonship. Maybe at long last we can move beyond the inadequate plans of salvation to the one revealed by our master.

9 Immortality

One of the more persistent questions among human beings has been, 'If a man die shall he live again?' In more modern form the question may be phrased differently. Dead and buried, is that the end? Is there anything left after the biological event we call death? Can any part of the human consciousness effectively separate itself from the physical entity we call the body? These are ancient questions that have echoed through the centuries. Humans have sought answers for ages and beliefs about some kind of life after death are the oldest known concepts of the human mind.

Neandertal beings lived from 100,000 to 250,000 years ago. They buried their dead with reverence, which indicates something about their thoughts of life and death. In ancient Persia, 70,000 years ago, people were buried with care in special places, with flowers to express love and grain to provide food for the next life. Some of the most towering monuments created by the hands of men, pyramids in Africa and South America, show physical evidence of beliefs in life after death.

In the culture into which Christianity was born there were well developed ideas about immortality. One of us lived for several months near the Greek temple in Eleusis where the rites of the Eleusenian mysteries were performed, all centred upon survival of physical death. Most ancient religions centred their ideas on the uniqueness of the human spirit, which had the capacity to survive physical cessation. The initial impetus of Christianity was bound up with the idea of resurrection. In a time when life was cheap, death common and human aspirations were discounted by a prevailing mood of despair, the promise of another life, where justice and love were paramount, must have had tremendous appeal.

69

In view of the persistence of ideas of immortality, it is important to try to separate the genuine human experience that underlies these ideas from the myths that have accreted about the ideas. Myths are important in creating the framework within which human experience can be understood. The facts of experience tend to remain the same but the myths can vary from age to age.

The idea of the resurrection is an example. There is little doubt that significant phenomena were experienced by the disciples. Jesus appeared to his disciples after his death. This verification of life after death was the foundation upon which the first century church was built. But the appearances were odd. His closest relatives and friends did not recognize him at first. He went through doors without opening them. He walked along the highway unrecognized by two close disciples. These seem to be the phenomena of experience. The disciples with their limited world view fitted them into what they knew of the rest of life and claimed the myth of physical resurrection.

Our world view would fit the phenomena into quite a different framework. Psychical research makes it clear that consciousness can live apart from the body in both time and space. The physical and spiritual bodies are different so this would account for some of the oddities of the phenomena. The emphasis on the physical and the material would be expected of the disciples, but not from Jesus. Out-of-body experiences and the presence of discarnate entities are the stuff of contemporary psychical research. And the myth of the ascension which is usually added to the myth of the resurrection would be possible with Ptolemaic cosmology but impossible with our world view. At thirty thousand feet a body would be frozen solid and at forty thousand plus it would explode from internal pressures in the rarified atmosphere. This would be quite different from sitting at the right hand of God, which would be acceptable in Ptolemaic terms, but unacceptable even to the nature of God revealed in the New Testament by Jesus. The revelation of Jesus in relation to the survival of physical death has suffered at the hands of reductionists as much as his other teachings about God, man and life.

Yet this history of Christendom has usually supported the untenable mythologies of the Ptolemaic perspective and ignored the wonder of the New Testament revelation. The reason for this seems to be that the demands of the New Testament revelation were so great that vigorous efforts were persistently made to avoid the full burden of responsibility and privilege implicit in the teachings of Jesus. The everyday orientation about the physical and material encourages a preoccupation with these elements of reality to the exclusion of the extrasensory, transpersonal, mystical and spiritual dimensions of our experience.

There seems to be a persistent interest among humans to assess the possibilities of their survival of bodily death. The thought that life may be brief and meaningless challenges something deep within the nature of consciousness. Paul Tillich claimed that the greatest source of human distress grew from death anxiety, often camouflaged or denied, but nonetheless showing up in forms of non-rational or bizarre behaviour in people and societies. Freud related this persistent quest to the characteristic of consciousness which at unconscious levels has no sense of time and space and so cannot imagine its own non-existence. Basically, the question concerning consciousness is, 'Does it verify itself in valid forms of reality perception, or is it an illusion growing from the peculiar qualities of consciousness itself?'

Contemporary thought has sought to answer this basic question in one of three ways: denial, extrapolation, or direct scientific research.

The materialist finds denial the only answer. The materialistic philosophy seeks to reduce human life to the level of a biological machine. Then the logical answer is quite simple. When the machine wears out or breaks down, it is finished. From this stance, to think of life after death is self-deception and to encourage such an idea is at best religious manipulation and at worst plain cruelty.

In recent years, physicians and others with important credentials as careful thinkers have observed phenomena that they think are significant and are extrapolating from them the answer 'perhaps' or 'maybe'. These answers coming from medicine and science are apt to be tentative and timid but represent quite a change in climate for the intellectual community. New scientific research into the nature of consciousness, as well as more recent concepts of science that equate reality with energy forms, has changed the focus from materialism to humanism with a new respect for spiritual aspects of being. Ancient ideas are being re-examined in a new context. Inquiry is taking place at new and different levels because new and different questions are being asked. Basically, the phenomena of consciousness that point in the direction of survival of consciousness are being treated as significant behaviour. Then the questions become, 'What does this behaviour mean? What does it tell us about human consciousness? What does it tell us about the energy of consciousness that may survive the biological event of organic disfunction we call death?'

Among those who have engaged in extrapolation at this point, we find Arnold Toynbee, Raymond Moody and Elizabeth Kubler-Ross. Here the experience of clinical death has been examined to see what it may tell us about states of consciousness that exist when normal brain function is supposed to have ceased. It deals with the period of time between the pronouncement of clinical death and the restoration of consciousness through heroic medical resuscitation. In many recorded cases, the consciousness appears to move into a state where time and space do not exist in the normal manner and euphoric states of being are experienced. But clinical death is not real death. In a Boston hospital, Kastenbaum interviewed many patients who had gone through the clinical death experience and found few who had any unusual experience of consciousness let alone the euphoric state. Does such research lead towards valid conclusions or does it nourish illusory states of perception?

Philosophers of science and researchers in parapsychology are bringing together other perceptions which may prove to be more valid and support the most audacious assumptions of the human spirit. Here the research moves at three levels. One is philosophical speculation to establish rational roots for the understanding of the nature of consciousness. The second is a form of self-criticism by scientists of the scientific method that has been traditionally employed but which tends to eliminate much human experience as anecdotal and unrepeatable in a laboratory. The third is the scientific study of consciousness to try to discover its nature, limits and boundaries.

Philosophers of science like Henry Margenau start with an examination of the energy of consciousness. If no other form of energy is ever destroyed, why would the energy of consciousness be the only energy form in all creation to be subject to destruction? If energy survives all forms of change, what happens to the energy of consciousness?

How does it continue to manifest itself? Newtonian physics, with its built-in space-time frame, made death philosophically rational, but in energy physics, which moves beyond a space-time frame, where does death go? Is death an illusion measured by the limits of sensory perception? When the philosopher of science speaks of the sixth dimension as the eternity dimension, he is not talking about religion in the strict sense, but about old ideas in a new framework. He is speaking of the infinite and the eternal as a scientific reality and not a religious assumption or a promise by a religious institution which enters into a bargaining arrangement with its communicants.

Philosophers of science are taking a hard look at scientific method to see what it ignores about human experience just because it cannot be fitted into preconceived methods of exploration. The entire spring issue (1978) of the *Journal of the American Academy of the Arts and Sciences* was given over to an assessment of the inadequacies of scientific inquiry. When science is so beset by methodological determinants that it ignores human and ethical considerations, it tends to become a restraint on truth rather than the source of it. When it comes to the exploration of the matters involved in research on survival, the new mood of scientific inquiry may open doors that before were closed or left just slightly ajar.

A new breed of scientists is looking with candour and objectivity at the phenomena that indicate there is a valid basis for believing that consciousness survives death. Dr Lawrence LeShan has spent twenty-five years exploring consciousness and its many manifestations in healing and survival. As a cancer research specialist, he first became interested through an awareness of the phenomena of spontaneous regressions. There was ample evidence of its existence in clinical studies, but there seemed to be a strange reticence in trying to understand what it means.

After years of study of the varied phenomena of consciousness, Dr LeShan wrote two books that have become the basis for most of the serious research in the boundaries of consciousness. In *The Medium, the Mystic and the Physicist* (Ballantine Books 1975), he looks at three different but valid ways of looking at reality. In his book *Alternative Realities* (Evans 1976) he tries to understand the larger picture of the reality perceived by consciousness by opening the doors wider to the

73

inventive-creative power of the mind that leads to fuller spirituality. In this fuller state, survival is achieved as the end result of disciplined and developed mental and spiritual resources. What he discovers in a scientific context is not far from the basic assumptions of the religious spirit. In fact he discovers new evidence to support ancient assumptions. What is the new evidence? How valid is it?

This evidence comes from several sources. During a sojourn in Iceland, we were intrigued to find an essentially communist government with spiritualism as the most prevalent religious choice. When the Professor of Psychiatry at the Medical School in Reykjavik was questioned about this, he responded that it might seem strange to others but in Iceland the traditions supported it. He then said that the main form of communication at a distance for centuries was controlled out of body travel where people would deliberately materialize themselves at another place.

Dr Ian Stevenson, Professor of Psychiatry at the University of Virginia medical school, after studying the experience of people in India of personality transplants in so-called reincarnation, wrote in the *Journal of Nervous and Mental Disease* (1977), 'The evidence of human survival after death is strong enough to permit a belief in survival.' Robert Laidlaw, for years chief of psychiatry at Roosevelt Hospital in New York, said that people who believe in immortality or survival make better progress in psychotherapy than those who do not. While this in itself is not proof, it does affirm the impact on consciousness of such beliefs. Instead of being illusory, they appear to be self-verifying in related forms of behaviour.

Sir John Eccles, the famous brain surgeon, in his Eddington Memorial lecture said:

I believe that the primary reality of my experiencing self cannot with propriety be identified with brains, neurons, nerve impulses or spatial temporal patterns of impulses . . . I cannot believe that the gift of conscious experience has no further future, no possibility of another existence under some other intangible conditions. At least I would maintain that this possibility of a future existence cannot be denied on scientific grounds.

These are quite different answers to the question of survival than those coming from materialistic and reductionist sources. Are they good enough answers to incorporate into one's philosophy of life? It now looks as if attitude is quantitative as well as qualitative. It may well be that beliefs make the life rather than the other way around. Two researchers, Gertrude Schmeidler, a psychologist, and R. A. McConnell, a physicist, in their findings published by Yale University Press, have proved that belief can be measured under laboratory controlled conditions and that believing has a bearing on mental and emotional behaviour. They also discovered that doubt is measurable as well and produces negative results in testing that are about equal to the positive results with believers. So if the mind's function as an inventive-creative resource is to create positive affirmations to support life, why not affirm the most life supporting and audacious beliefs possible?

When one speaks at conferences on consciousness and its functions and asks how many believe in immortality, few raise their hands. Follow this by asking how many have had paranormal experiences and the response is often nearly unanimous. New words carry new meanings and the exploration of consciousness in depth makes the unusual forms of knowing that come with clairvoyance, telepathy and precognition quite clearly evidence of survival that is more resonant to minds trained in science more than in religion. Immortality is the religious word. Survival of consciousness is the scientific terminology. If the consciousness can move ahead in time, perceive without normal sensory involvement and know with assurance what is unsupported by the evidence of eye or ear, we are talking about the phenomena that have puzzled humans from the beginning of time.

Yet we are looking at these same phenomena from a different perspective and with different laws of evidence. Instead of being frightened, we are intrigued. Instead of being overcome with religious fervour, we are consumed with scientific interest. Instead of running away from this dimension of our experience, we are facing it to see what it can tell us about ourselves and the structure of the universe we inhabit. These are, in a sense, the affirmations of faith that come from a new idea of the nature of consciousness, a new awareness of laws of the universe just being discovered. It may well be the most challenging and creative frontier of research opened up in our century.

We spent billions on a flight to the moon which found a dead celestial body. The journey into the depths of consciousness is finding new and amazing powers in humans which may be so alive that they survive the death of the body itself.

The current interest in meditation, the extrasensory and the paranormal has become a legitimate area of research. If we can discover how these journeys of the mind in and out of space-time help us understand the inventive-creative power of the mind, we may be on the verge of a breakthrough in self-understanding that can affect health, self-esteem, personal and social motivation. It may lay a new basis for inter-relation, personally, socially and internationally, for we all may realize that we are bound together in a psychic force field that surmounts all old and superficial and conflicting boundaries. We may well find the key to a new type of relationship to each other, wherever we are and whatever language we speak.

If we are preoccupied with preserving old modes of thinking about life and death, heaven and hell, salvation and damnation, we are trying to fit human experience into the outworn concept of the nature of humans and the cosmos. But if we take the experience of the ancients and understand it in terms of newly discovered resources of consciousness, we may verify the old and build it into a new understanding of how the consciousness works and how its energy not only affirms the experiences of the past that have been so baffling, but even more may lay the foundation for a great leap into the future towards what Pierre Teilhard calls the *omega* man.

When that happens, we will not only find that belief in survival of bodily death, or immortality if you choose, is not only possible, but essential to healthy religious attitudes. Healthy religion stimulates growth. Unhealthy religion inhibits the development of understanding of the self, of others and the universe of law and order in which we live and move and have our being. The current interest in a careful and disciplined study of the phenomena of the consciousness at work can open the door for new growth, new faith and new confidence in the power within us.

The older ideas of reward and punishment, related to the institutional concept of survival, may have impaired the sensitivity of spirit and freedom of consciousness to develop its own inner depths of being.

This being is the place where the belief is nourished which can produce the inventive-creative perceptions that are the best guarantee of a healthfully developed spirit. If reality is to be experienced fully, it must be within the growth of the inner being that can be fully aware. It cannot be administered from outside by those who would manipulate the emotions for purposes of self-interest or institutional power over the lives of others.

We are entering a new day. Dr Rhine at Duke University, North Carolina, claims that he has proved within the laboratory that immortality as we define it clearly exists and is a demonstrable fact. The most audacious assumptions of Christendom have affirmed such an estimate of the potential of human personality. Now we can bring together the finest aspirations of the past and the richest assumptions of the present to support the meaning of our present existence by the affirmation of our spiritual survival as an acceptable product of the newer and greater reality we can know. Think what that great affirmation can do for a day that has lost its spiritual horizons, its sense of great purpose and its acceptance of great religious assurances about life and death. In a different way, we may be experiencing what the first century called the resurrection.

10 The Ideal and the Actual

An objective of religion is to promote ideals. In recent years Western idealism has weakened and now needs to be revived.

Ideals take many forms. Some have to do with making a living, raising a family, serving altruistic causes, promoting the values of truth and beauty, or leading a deeply religious life. The human of the species has more needs and aspirations than any other creature; hence, it is not surprising that he has trouble living with his inevitable disappointments. Nearly everyone has aspirations and ideals – at least of the minimal kind – and literally everyone suffers disappointments in achieving these ideals. Jesus was mindful of this problem and spoke concerning it frequently.

There is a close connection between ideals and the idea of perfection. Jesus tended to use the two terms interchangeably, especially when dealing with the religious life: 'Be thou therefore perfect, even as your Father in Heaven is perfect.' Jesus was an idealist. He never lost sight of his ultimate goals and never compromised in their attainment. At the same time, he realized how human we are and how difficult it is, if not impossible, to be consistent all the time. Consequently, unlike the Pharisees, whom he continually belaboured, Jesus' idealism did not focus on outward observances to the exclusion of human sympathy and understanding. Idealism, to him, was the spirit of love, not impeccable imitation of others and their superficial conventions.

When one speaks of perfect love or a perfect religious life, however, as Jesus continually did, it becomes necessary to have more than a superficial acquaintance with the idea of perfection as Jesus used it. The dictionary tells us that perfection is something that is thoroughly made or formed and that, equally, is carried out or done. This provides an important clue as to what kind of ideal it is to which we should aspire. Perfection is a lovely face from which kindness and helpfulness to others shines forth. It is a hand that an artist would wish to draw and that at the same time succours the needy.

We stress these two aspects of perfectionism, the form and the deed, because in the juxtaposition of these two inter-related halves is found the key to most of the disagreements that idealists have quarrelled over since the time of Plato in the fifth century before the birth of Christ.

The earliest conception of idealism, which was Plato's, held that for everything in the universe there is a perfect idea or form and that this ideal is not man-made but inherent. The form exists in nature and all creation. Later, during the Reformation, the viewpoint developed that the ideal is created by the activity of the human mind, which learns to recognize the ideal outside oneself and make it part of the individual's and the group's experience. More recently, the ideal is regarded as something that evolves, that may be lost sight of temporarily, but that re-emerges and is added to as individuals attempt to make it better than it has been before.

Idealism, in short, consists of those profound spiritual insights, experiences and inner voices that pervade and inspire the progressively improving nature of the individual's being. Hence, from the time of Plato, through the ruminations of Hegel, Kant, Berkeley, Emerson, Royce and a host of philosopher-thinkers, we have come full circle to Jesus' belief that perfection is equally form and doing, the outward expression fired by the inner spirit.

Looking at the matter in terms of what you and I experience, we find that it is apparently normal for most people to have ideals or standards of excellence early in life. We can all think of dozens of examples. A boy wants to become a doctor and seems to have all the natural aptitudes. But his father dies young and the boy never finishes high school. His sister is maternal and desires a large family. She has an unfortunate love affair and winds up wrapping packages in a department store. Or an able Senator aspires to the Presidency and his son's escapades, which make front page news, remove him from all consideration. Some of these ideals and aspirations may sound like dreams and fantasies. Perhaps, but they are all of a piece. They are all mystical experiences, aspirations, yearnings at the heart of religious experience.

Not everyone has the same ideals, of course, any more than they have the same goals and objectives. For every person or institution, it might be possible to devise a hierarchy of ideals, with certain ultimate values such as justice and the sanctity of life at the top. The simple fact is that everyone has dreams of one kind or another and if religion were more effective, more people would dream and more dreams could be realized.

It is a universal experience that often the peak of one's dreaming period is found in one's younger years. There is doubtless a physiological foundation for this, but it is also explained by the fact that the child is more natural and unaffected than he will be later and less influenced by the buffetings and disappointments bearing in upon him from the social environment. He has not yet been made to conform to adult expectations and disillusionments. Merely to see a bird in flight makes a child think immediately of his soaring towards the skies. To listen to a musical score sounds like the constellation of the stars transporting him into space and brings forth ecstasy and an instinctive tear of joy. To see a baby in a cradle means holding it in one's arms as one's own. Christ said children are nearer to heaven than at most times after they become older and are less emotional and dream less. We say that everyone needs to be 'socialized'. If we worked equally hard to keep individuals natural, spontaneous and sincere, they might be nearer to the ideal than those who show the chisel marks of social moulding.

But it is a sober fact that few of us ever realize our ideals, or achieve them fully. This stern reality has been well expressed by Theodore Parker Ferris, a Boston clergyman, in these words:

[Human beings] seldom, if ever, grasp the things they reach for. Their ideal home life and their actual home life are often poles apart. Their ideal political society and their actual political society . . . are often as different as night and day. Their ideal characters, the men [and women] they would be . . . seem to bear little resemblance to each other. There is always a gulf between the ideal and the actual. In life as we know it there is always a discrepancy, and sometimes an enormous one, between what ought to be and what is.

The easy thing to do is give up the ideal and become complacent.

As might be expected, it has occurred to some thinkers through the centuries that if society tends to frustrate youthful idealism, then the rational solution is to mould society in such a way that most young dreamers need not be disappointed any more. Actually, every society, including our own, has experienced some effects of this line of reasoning.

In our case, we stress freedom of opportunity, equality under the law and civil liberties generally. But although these are clearly standards and standards are a synonym for ideals, ordinarily we do not attempt to force everyone into a common mould. We create the rules and the parameters, but stop short of trying to change human nature. However, in certain other countries they go beyond this – they do attempt to change human nature because they consider that their ideal justifies it. Such indoctrination is practiced in the Soviet Union, mainland China under Mao, Castro's Cuba and many other countries where various communist ideologies are to be found. All such countries trace their lineage back to idealists such as Hegel, who owed his own intellectual heritage to Plato.

Does the fact that idealists have been instrumental in influencing political systems we do not favour mean that the less we have to do with idealists, the better? Such a conclusion is unfortunate because it is unjustified. Ideals hold societies together. If people do not think about a good and just society, they are not likely to achieve it. Nor is the Christian religion of love, peace and good works likely to be achieved if we do not believe in these ideals and work to attain them. In other words, the conformity inherent in communism is not inherent in ideals. If conformity is inherent at all, it is in the methods employed. The ideal is a liberator, not a jailer.

There are, of course, varying degrees of coercion and inducement that political systems can use in order to promote social ideals. In a democracy, the carrot is preferred to the stick. The ideal political system promotes ideals but also diversity. It believes in consensus freely arrived at. People are happier and develop better when they act out of voluntary incentive instead of fear. This does not mean that there are no things about human nature in high and low places in the Western world that do not need changing. Human nature is essentially good, but develops excesses and pathologies, and it is a function of religion to correct these imbalances.

An ideal is a personal thing and precious. If it is excessively institutionalized and forced into a common mould, one may get the outward form but lose the underlying spirit. No ideal is worth pursuing if it does not feed the spirit. People have lived for decades – even centuries – with a smouldering sense of injustice, awaiting only the proper moment to set things right. Ideals are as tough and durable as the granite face on a mountain.

There is no such thing as a happy society if individuals are denied the right to seek happiness in their own way. And once force and compulsion are used to achieve what individuals seek through spiritual insight and experience, in effect religion is undermined at its very source.

Equally, it would be a mistake to assume that society ought not to be improved. Although it is unfortunately true that most people are more idealistic and hence happier when they are young than they are when they become older, the solution to this is found in Jesus' teaching: love your neighbour; abide by the law; do not deviate from high standards of ethics; see God in nature; denounce hypocrisy and sham sentiments of piety; contribute to society; speak out for truth and goodness; develop leadership in all institutions of life, beginning with the church itself. Christianity, more than any other faith, is a religion of activism and reform.

The ultimate truth about idealism is that it is personal, precious and self-contained. It is personhood. It is spiritual growth. It is the inner joy that comes from feeling that ideals gradually grow despite vicissitudes and setbacks. The inner life becomes stronger and more rewarding because it is a combination of testing and gaining, failure and success, becoming more humble as one becomes more attuned to God. It is the still small voice within.

The most interesting idealists are those who seem to have been born that way. There were many of them in my college, because it was a college that had emblazoned on its gates, 'Our tribute to Christian civilization', and a sort of natural selection seemed to take place. However, the children of idealists do not necessarily become idealists. Even in the same family, one child may be highly idealistic and another the opposite extreme. Idealists are more often badly treated than those who are more calculating and self-centred. Sometimes people take idealism as a form of weakness and treat the idealist accordingly. But many idealists have remained idealists all their lives and to do this they had to be 'tough', in the sense that they never forsook that which came naturally to them and hence was the core of their being. We should treat such people with great respect, because it takes courage and will-power to be an idealist in any age, and perhaps especially so in ours.

Whether one speaks of the kingdom of God or of Utopia, it does not come all at once. It comes gradually. There are reverses and heart-breaks. We need to be clear, therefore, about the process as well as the terminal.

There are so many little things that we can do if we keep our eyes open for the opportunity. And the total of these little things, if fully examined and evaluated, often exceeds the total of what another in-dividual accomplishes in some sensational achievement that reaches the headlines. It is the analogue of the aphorism 'Little streams do mighty oceans make.'

Anthropologists have increasingly discovered that man rises from one plateau to another, sometimes painfully and haltingly. The same thing seems to apply to the individual. His confidence and idealism exhibit spurts of vitality as success is attained. The spirit declines when adversity is a sufficient damper. During periods of inertia or depression, there are two rules of life that it pays to keep activated: as long as the spirit is warm, the vitality is still there and once a plateau has been attained, there is a certainty that one can, at the least, re-attain the heights that have been lost. The spirit fans the flame and once the spirit is revived, the little achievements that add up to large totals can again be reinstituted. In most people, therefore, idealism is evolutionary. It occurs most frequently when through experience we learn to combine the ideal and the actual.

For the past forty years, most of the testimony of social scientists has been to the effect that idealism, as a philosophical school of doc-trine, is dead. But I wonder if it is? One gets the impression that in the sixteen to twenty-one age group today there is as much under-lying idealism as there was in the period after World War I. It is possible that what is needed, therefore, is a new distillation and definition of idealism. What is needed is a new emphasis that will make idealism relevant and challenging again. Once the notion is abandoned that all ideals lead inevitably to authoritarianism, perhaps the transition can be made. One facet of this missing dimension is unquestionably the idea of perfection that Jesus stressed so much in his teaching and his daily example.

Moreover, in nature, those individuals who do not adapt to the laws of the universe which end in perfection, soon die. Perhaps, now that food and energy are both relatively in shorter supply worldwide, man's intelligence will persuade a new generation that the ramifications of natural law for *homo sapiens* are not so different.

Again, the extreme notion of a superior race and of purity of the blood line, as advocated in the Hitler period, clearly ought to be rejected. But this does not dispose of the older and deeper question raised by the Greek philosophers, namely the desirability of improving the human stock by natural means. Because of advances in medicine and in religious sentiment, the danger today is that the least capable of survival will increase proportionally in number to the population as a whole, while the most advantaged, from an heriditary standpoint, may decline. The marginal or submarginal reproduce in large numbers while the healthier and better educated ones do not. To neglect the disadvantaged is clearly morally wrong, but equally to neglect the more promising genes and chronosomes is equally wrong. The genetic ideal should be improvement, not retrogression.

Another facet of a new idealism arises at just this point. The first law of the universe is creativity. If idealism is to attain a more durable foundation, therefore, creativity in its manifold dimensions may provide the essential ingredient. Man has a great potential that he has never fully developed. This philosophy of science holds that man's highest obligation is to understand the spirit and principles that the creator breathed into the universe and then accept the responsibility for developing new and better order ourselves. It is an appeal to reason and known facts. It bridges the gulf between capitalist and communist doctrines. We live partial lives now. But once we have developed a fully-fledged philosophy of creativity, there is no reason why we should not be able to achieve greatly enriched lives.

Religion, in the transcendental sense, is more than doctrine and cult. It is a reaching out for universal ideals. And these ideals are realized by combining the twin halves of perfection and creativity, as the union of man and woman creates new life.

11 Health

There has long been an assumption that there is an active relationship between religion and the organic behaviour we call illness. A prominent activity of the New Testament was the healing of people's miseries of body, mind and spirit. And the inter-relation between body and attitudes is implicit in the words that Jesus repeated again and again, 'Your faith has made you whole.'

In more than half of the reported healing incidents in the New Testament, the only process evident was the restoration of faith, a changed attitude towards the self and life. Jesus never denied the reality of disease. He never called it an illusion, as is the case with Christian Science. Rather, he faced the reality of organic breakdown and dis-ease with another resource that was so strong that it could overcome the effects of organic failure.

In our age of intensive medical research, this New Testament stance is finding significant support. The most active support for holistic medicine is coming from psychosomatic research done largely by physicians themselves. The tradition of modern medicine has been largely materialistic, with the human body treated as a machine or chemical factory. If the machine is in trouble and malfunctioning, it is referred to as a breakdown. The medical mechanic may remove or replace the malfunctioning part, with little interest or concern about the cause-effect factors that may be responsible for the breakdown.

Perhaps this traditional stance has been most actively expressed in the treatment of cancer. The three modes of medical intervention with cancer have been to cut it out, burn it out or poison it to death; more specifically, surgery to excise the offending tissue, radiation

87

to burn out the weak and purposeless cells and chemotherapy to poison the weak cells. Yet, as we will point out later, of all diseases, cancer seems to be the most easily demonstrated to be psychogenic or psychosomatic. That means that it tends to be a body metaphor, an effort of the body to tell us something about its response to emotional and environmental stresses. This is based on the assumption that each person is a major environmental factor in life.

The materialistic trend in medical practice that has been centred about surgical modification or change in the chemistry of the body has been confronted in recent years by the assumption that all behaviour is meaningful and that organic behaviour is no exception. If all disease is an effect, then it is essential to discover the causes in order to effectively treat the organic acting out of that causal relationship. To this end, Dr Jerome Frank of Johns Hopkins Medical School suggests that no physician prescribe medicine unless he first establishes the placebo response of the patient, lest the medical intervention disturb the body chemistry and actively interfere with the body's immunological resources.

The history of psychosomatic research has been interesting. It has been opposed by physicians who feel that it may challenge their authority, even though they may indirectly employ its resources in what is referred to as bedside manner. Courageous and innovative physicians have found it difficult to ignore the cause–effect factors that they have observed in their practice.

Dr Walter Cannon, a professor at the Harvard Medical School, became so interested in the wonders of body chemistry and its relationship to immunological processes that he wrote a classic book called *The Wisdom of the Body* (W. W. Norton 1980). In this book, he explores the wonders of the glandular system and its constant activity in maintaining a balance between warmth and cooling, between too much or too little of glandular secretion to maintain the digestive process and the control or reaction to the environment. He was fascinated with kidneys and their millions of built in computers that are constantly monitoring and controlling the chemical needs of the body.

In a second book, Dr Cannon ties his theories more closely to emotional states of the individual. In *Bodily Changes in Pain, Hunger,*

Fear and Rage (Harper 1963), he details research that shows how emotional states may actively modify such body functions as digestion and metabolism. In these books, Dr Cannon gives a more precise and authoritative definition of causal relationships that had long been observed but little explored or understood.

A remarkable woman named Flanders Dunbar became fascinated with the work of Dr Cannon. She carried it further. After getting degrees in psychology, philosophy, medicine and religion, she gained a diploma in psychiatry and then went to work to find out all she could about coordinating the cause-effect processes in medical research.

Dr Dunbar wrote the classic work in the field of psychogenic and psychomatic medicine, *Emotions and Bodily Changes* (Columbia 1956). In this work she correlates various diseases and the emotional states that might appear to be etiologically significant. Every aspect of disease is examined to see if cause-effect factors can be isolated and attributed to disturbances of the emotions. There appears to be an almost unfailing link between what is going on in the emotional life of an individual and what is being acted out metaphorically in the body structure.

When one of us was teaching in the paramedical department of the Mayo Hospital in Minnesota, he became aware of another research that carried a step further the perceptions of Cannon and Dunbar. Patients coming in for a thorough check-up were requested to send in two weeks before admission the detailed description of two recent dreams. These were turned over to a specialist in dream analysis to see what this metaphor of the unconscious might be saying. A diagnosis was made from the dream content and placed in the medical records file. Only after the patient had been put through a battery of diagnostic tests physically was the medical diagnosis compared with the diagnoses made from the content of dreams. On comparison, it was found that there was a striking similarity in the two diagnoses, but also it was found that the dreams revealed some things that the physical examinations had failed to show and so more exploration was made to verify the correlation of the dream metaphors with the body metaphors. It became clear from this research that all there is of a person is unified in the wholeness of being. Beyond the denials and the efforts to camouflage emotional states, their integrity cannot be violated; and body, mind and spirit are bound in an inseparable unity. One cannot reasonably treat any one part of a person without paying attention to all the rest of that person. It sounds strangely like the New Testament, doesn't it?

· More recently, one of us worked with Dr Lawrence LeShan on a book called *You Can Fight for your Life* (Evans 1977). For a quarter of a century, Dr LeShan has been researching the dynamics of spontaneous regressions in cancer cases. The more study he did, the more it became clear that the cancer was often the acting out in bodily form of the emotional states that possessed a person deep in the recesses of their inner being. In fact, Dr LeShan said that the major emotional state of the cancer patient is a mood of 'bleak and unutterable despair', the loss of hope and meaning for life. This often follows an acute loss such as that which comes with the death of an important person in one's life pattern. It may also come with burning emotions like intense guilt, or response to overwhelming failure, or life-shattering compromise.

Dr LeShan was asked to explain to me in simple terms the dynamic process that appeared to be present in this cause-effect relationship in the development and also the cure of cancer. He pointed out the basic chain of relationship in this manner. First, the emotions most immediately affect the glandular system. We are aware of the instant response of the various glands to emotional stimulae. The lacrimator glands, the salivary glands, the sex glands and the glands of the skin can react instantly to our feelings and whatever activates them. He pointed out further that the glands are the chemical factories of the body and also that a major portion of cancers begin in the glands of the body. The glands as the source of body chemistry control the immunological systems of the body. When the body experiences imbalance of body chemistry, two things may happen. There may be a breakdown in the control of cell division. There may also be a failure of the body to control viral developments. In simple terms, a cold may follow fatigue. In complex forms, uncontrolled cell division may allow malignant growth forms to achieve an accelerated role in body function.

If cancer is to be effectively treated, it seems important to marshal the healthy forces of the being to support the normal immunological processes within the body to supplement any other treatment modality that may be employed. It becomes equally obvious that if the preventive stance against cancer is to be fully developed, it must take into account the emotional factors that are part of the cause-effect chain in the development of neoplastic tissue.

It is interesting to note that the usually conservative American Medical Association has accepted a report at its annual convention a few years ago asserting that all disease is psychosomatic. Drs Lawrence E. Hinkle Jr and Horald G. Wolff of New York Hospital and Cornell Medical Center state that there is no aspect of the body system which is not influenced by the brain's effort to adapt and that bodily processes changed by mental activity may lead to serious physical damage. Their judgment, based on five years of research, makes it clear that 'man's attempt to adapt to his social environment is a very important determinant of his health in general, which often overrides all other influences – a matter which must be of ever-increasing concern to medicine in years to come.'

In the two volume work *Medical Research*, there are two rather startling sentences: 'A change at one point, in one molecule even, may reverberate throughout the entire system to initiate changes in seemingly unrelated organs and tissues. This concept, familiar in physics, is gaining validity in all fields of biology and medicine.'

Where does this lead us? If intense concentration can start thousands of molecules in motion in any given second and if emotional thinking of the negative or destructive kind can start reverberations through our whole system, we quickly become aware of the importance of right thoughts and feelings. If one hundred per cent of all illness is psychosomatic, we move into the centre of the picture of the prevention, control and cure of the ailments so much a part of our human experience.

Little things begin to take on great importance. We are not certain that anyone has ever seen a molecule. Using the electron microscope, infinitessimal forms can be seen that we assume are molecules. But we can be sure that the flow of these minute particles affect our health profoundly. You can begin to see how significantly this new approach to health puts us and our theology of relevance at the centre of the picture.

91

For years we have been able to escape responsibility for our own health by making the physician the scapegoat. We expect him to do our work for us, just as we avoid moral responsibility by creating a cosmic scapegoat that we call our God. If health and personal wholeness are the end result of perceptions that are within our control, we cannot escape our responsibility for self-discipline and responsible control of our life style and our life attitudes.

We cannot deny the personal responsibility related to both social and personal patterns of living and emotional expression. Dr James Lynch of Johns Hopkins medical school has written a book on *The Broken Heart: Medical Consequences of Loneliness* (Basic Books 1978) in which he gives clear medical evidence of the life destroying influence of separation, isolation and fractured human contact. People actually die of these painful emotions. Our society tends to compound the problem by easy family breakup and impersonal urban crowding. People need people in sickness and in health and we cannot escape the obligations of our humanity by encouraging various forms of separation and retreat from our fellow creatures.

Dr Ronald Glazer, the Professor of Internal Medicine at the University of Minnesota Medical School, has written a book entitled *Our Greatest Battle*. In it he points out that the greatest medical problem of our day is cigarette smoking, which kills three hundred thousand people each year in usually agonizing forms of disease like choking to death with emphysema or lung cancer. Yet this form of self-destructive behaviour is brashly advertised in magazines and newspapers, and this form of death is for sale at grocery stores, supermarkets and even drug stores in America. The issue which once seemed to be related to personal preference and individual freedom of choice has now become one of the major moral problems of our day. There seems to be no rational warrant for this intense form of air pollution and life-destroying drug addiction. Just because it is popular does not make it exempt from our concerns about moral responsibility and healthful behaviour.

We know too well that there are hereditary, environmental, accidental and aging factors that affect our health, but we know also that attitudes are related to all of the health impairing processes that touch our lives. The way we feel about ourselves and the ways we use to respond to other people are constantly at work to produce the inner changes that make people well or make them sick. We determine what the impact of our lives will be. The Old Testament concern about being our brother's keeper has a more positive emphasis in the New Testament. We cannot escape our responsibility to others. In fact, Jesus makes it clear that right relations with others is a prerequisite even to worship. If we cannot love our fellow men, how can we love God?

The basic elements of a theology of relevance come to life in a special way when we think of the relation of religion to health. In a day when the major expense for human services is a medical one, we are making great investment in the physical aspects of health. It does not make sense to ignore the major factor producing disease by irresponsible and anti-social behaviour. Most of us are endowed with marvellous bodies that serve us well through many years. We are placed together in families and societies that can enrich life with meaning and companionship. It is unreasonable to destroy life and health by supporting the forms of behaviour that are personally and socially destructive. We cannot escape responsibility for our health even though we might want to. Years ago, Samuel Butler wrote a book called *Erewhon* – which reads 'nowhere' backwards (Heron Books 1978). It was a social exploration of human behaviour. In that book, he makes a strange suggestion, that sick people should be punished and criminals should be treated. In his book, *The Crime of Punishment*, Karl Menninger says that our penal system works overtime to create criminals. And the church rewards people for being sick and passes cruel judgment on those who threaten our security by violating the law. Perhaps we need to re-examine various forms of significant behaviour in the light of the New Testament and its teachings.

A theology of relevance calls for responsibility, discipline, inspiration that leads to implementation and personal and social fulfilment. It seems to be clear that in our search for health the same basic attitudes are essential. We cannot blame others for the conditions we create. If we develop the religious attitudes that foster faith, hope and love, we will eliminate hate, despair and fearfulness. We will do our part to verify the research in psychosomatic ailments

93

by projecting the more abundant life in our bodies, our thoughts and our emotions. Then our faith will have a chance to make us whole.

12 Religion and the Problem of Suffering

Suffering has been a constant of the human condition. So, quite naturally, suffering has been a central concern of religion. Most world religions have sought to understand suffering, relieve suffering and explain suffering. Some of the explanations have been bizarre efforts to attribute cosmic meaning to suffering and make a punitive God the cause of the human plight. At its best, Christianity has tried to separate God from any causal relationship to human distress. The gospel assures us that it is not God's will that one of his creatures should suffer. But the suffering does exist and the search for answers that makes sense continues.

Pain and suffering impair life. The world of the person in intense pain of long duration is apt to be a constantly narrowing world, restricting life and its perspectives. The end result may be a person who has reduced the meaning of life to little more than the relationship between the suffering and the self. So there has been a long tradition of efforts to relieve suffering. Primitive people ate weeds that reduced the consciousness of pain. More contemporary medical practice has refined the methods but uses the same plants and their extracts to limit painful experience. Yet the side effects of pain limiting drugs may produce a dependency that is as difficult to manage as the pain itself.

Two recent developments tend to move pain intervention away from chemicals and back toward religious presuppositions. They assume that the person and the attitudes of the person are a major consideration in solving the riddle of pain. Drs Elmer and Alice

Greene of the Menninger Clinic find that pain can be reduced or eliminated by altering the state of consciousness. Pain appears to exist only in one level of consciousness. By training a person to control the level of awareness, there may be movement from one set of brain waves where pain is experienced to another set of brain waves where pain is not experienced. This phenomenon has long been observed in practical form, for example, a person takes a nap when a headache occurs and the headache disappears. Modern methods are able to increase purposive control of thought patterns to relieve pain.

This deliberate control of inner states has long been a form of religious intervention. Reduce anger and find inner peace and you feel better. Anger increases blood flow and causes congestion in the brain. Relaxation, change of thought focus and restoration of inner peace may have demonstrable results and the forms of behaviour modification, long a part of religious exercises, have another demonstrably valid function in pain modification.

Within the last three or four years, there has been a marked interest in chemical functions in the brain. This has centred on the production of peptides called endorphins. It appears that the brain can produce molecules that control pain. Certain conditions encourage the production of endorphins. Quiet and peaceful states of mind appear to encourage this production just as tension and stress inhibit the pain relieving process. Much that is a part of modern life tends to be pain-producing and it seems important to rediscover the processes by which inner distress can be ameliorated.

But, lest we take too narrow an approach to pain and suffering, we need to recognize that the human organism is the focal point for a variety of pain-producing agents. The skin is a sensory organ that shuts the creature in and protects it from the outside world. But the task of marking this boundary between the two worlds is apt to be a frontier where skirmishes are constant. Insects, fungi and climatic forces are constantly at work. People live in parched deserts and frigid climates. The distress of the body in these conditions is a warning of the need for protection and relief from the assaults from outside.

Also it is obvious that pain can be inflicted deliberately. Not only do we have the emotionally disturbed, who act out their abnormality through sadism and masochism, but also we have the social, religious and political sources of purposeful pain. The cruelty that leads to torture, the religious ideas that lead to persecution and the inquisitorial spirit, and the terrorism that seeks control through fear of injury, are well known in history and are still a part of contemporary life.

Social patterns produce guilt and judgment with the special form of suffering that comes with ostracism and incarceration. Other forms of distress come from changes that disrupt life such as illness and death. When we identify with the lives of others, what happens to them also happens to us. Also, political turmoil, social revolution and the disrupting of life inflict pain on untold millions of people constantly. The things we call evil, the natural catastrophies, floods, hurricanes and earthquakes, are sources of injury and suffering.

Because we are an important part of our own environment, what goes on within us can produce suffering. Depression, despair, guilt, grief and self-pity are constantly at work to disturb our balance in life. The illnesses that come from many sources, the environment without and within, the aging process, accidents and hereditary factors, are constantly at work to cause suffering. So we confront the many sources of distress without and within as a constant in our human experience.

We do not confront the various forms of suffering wisely unless we have a discriminating form of perception, for not all pain is the same. Some is meaningless and some is meaningful. Some bodily signals must be explored, for the messages they bring may be important to our total welfare. So a toothache sends us to the dentist for necessary repair and treatment. Visceral distress invites intervention from the skilled professional who guards our health. Human cruelty leads to social controls that can make life more secure. Much progress in architecture, agriculture, medicine and political science is designed to reduce human suffering. We want to hear the messages that lead to creative action at the same time that we want to protect ourselves and others from the kinds of cruel and disruptive behaviour that needlessly lay waste life.

How, then, does all of this effort to understand and control suffering fit into our religious explorations? Religion focuses on the answers for the basic question 'Why?' To this end it seeks meanings and tries to find wise and discriminating answers. It encourages insight and understanding where these seem elusive. It invites an examination of differing perspectives on the distressing aspects of human experience.

Man's long experience with pain and suffering has led to many and varied answers. 'My God, why?' has echoed through the centuries. Some people in response have said their distress was a warning or a punishment. Some have sought to reduce their pain through herbs and drugs. Some have tried to employ denial as if to say their pain was an illusion. Some have been moved to courageous action to eliminate the suffering. Others have tried to develop the inner resources to cope wisely with that which has destroyed their joy in living.

The classic answer of the Old Testament to the problem of suffering is found in the Book of Job. Here, in the mood of an ancient drama with characters presented in extravagant form, the plight of a suffering human is confronted. Job is injured in all of the ways the dramatist can imagine, with loss of children, personal wealth and status; he is also afflicted with physical distress, with boils from head to toe.

Job's friends, Eliphaz, Bildad and Zophar, sit in silence with Job for days, sharing his suffering. Then Bildad makes bold to speak with the suggestion that it may be that Job is suffering for secret sins or repressed emotions that are unhealthy. This is the method that might be employed by the psychologist or the pastoral counsellor. Job rejects this idea and clings to his feeling of blamelessness.

Bildad adds his thought that the suffering may be illusory and that if he just looked at the world through rose-coloured glasses, everything would appear better to him. This idea, too, Job rejects with disgust for he points out that he knows his suffering and no one outside of him can really understand the hurt.

Zophar adds his thought that suffering has to be expected for it is the kind of universe where sensitive beings are so vulnerable that there is really no escape. Job seems to think that this makes more sense than anything else that has been said and he responds positively.

However, it is at this point that the voice of youth is heard. Elihu indicates that he is disappointed in the views of his seniors for he thinks there is a much more positive approach that can be taken to suffering. Not in blind resignation, nor in subtle sophistries, would he find the answer. Rather he sees that suffering can be a doorway to growth and finer sensitivity, with a redemptive quality implicit in its nature. For him, suffering produces perspective, and perspective produces maturity and the movement beyond selfish preoccupation.

The climax of this wonderful drama comes when God speaks and challenges men to grow to the point where they can see life and the cosmic processes from God's unlimited point-of-view, rather than their own limited and limiting selfishness. This cosmic perspective opens the way for the ideas of the New Testament.

Jesus points out that pain and suffering are not necessarily the result of sin. When people get in the way of cosmic processes through ignorance or carelessness, they suffer the consequences, for the alternative of a capricious God, or a universe where the law and order were undependable, would be far more distressing. The concern, then, is to take what is and develop responsibility and understanding so that needless suffering is reduced and the openly accepted and purposeful suffering may have its best effect. This then becomes transforming suffering, accepted with willingness and used for purposes that are in accord with growth in responsibility.

Jesus seeks to help people discover both the meaning of their humanity and their mark of divinity. In his own life he showed that we are closest to God's purpose when we take the elements of our humanity that could lead to selfishness and triviality and direct the energies of life toward fulfilling the redemptive purposes of God. He used the laws of the universe to reveal the laws of the spirit. Never does Jesus deny the reality of suffering, but he seeks to give it a transcendent meaning. He activates the healing, redeeming love of the holy spirit, at work in life to release people from self-imposed and self-destructive suffering and find in its place the willingness to accept burdens and assume responsibility for others, so that all may move closer to that more abundant life that is the promise revealed by his life. In practical terms, Paul confronted the reality of suffering and the promise of comfort to those who sought meaning in their condition. But he went further. He felt suffering could be a gateway to the understanding of God's redemptive love at work, not through magic but through discipline. He emphasized the place of faith as the ingredient that made the purpose secure, for nothing that was done with God's will and purpose was ever wasted or lost. This assumption

99

undergirded life and its activities with an assurance that was constantly verifying itself. This idea moves far beyond the Old Testament idea that sin and suffering are related. In fact, the equating of sin and suffering makes the whole idea of man's sensitivity and the nature of the God-man relationship indefensible. Only when we are able to accept suffering as a resource for growth and healing of man and society can we understand the idea of glorification. In suffering to relieve suffering, we discover more than our distress; we discover the higher purposes of our humanity that bring us into active relationship with God. Then the cross becomes understandable.

It is difficult to understand and accept the cause-effect processes at work in much of human suffering. When people break out of socially accepted modes of behaviour, we are inclined to look at the behaviour rather than the frustration that causes people to become terrorists and use pain as a weapon. But we cannot think of the Palestine Liberation Organization without the thirty years of concentration camps for the Palestinian refugees that precipitated it. We cannot think of the terror in Nicaragua in 1978 without decades of repressive government. We cannot think of fourteen hundred and thirty nine bombings in America in one year without thinking of the injustices that lay behind them. This in no way justifies terrorism with its suffering, but it confronts the cause-effect processes at work leading to this type of non-rational action.

Similarly, it is difficult to look at the breakdown of an individual in emotional or physical illness without taking into account the prolonged stresses and acute pain which became so intolerable that organized and effective living collapsed and the afflicted person became non-functional. When one of us was chaplain in a hospital for 2,800 mental cases, it was distressing to see the endless line of people who had not been able to develop the resources necessary to cope with life. One day, a psychiatrist said it was futile to treat these people and then send them out again into the families, the communities and the competitive society that had broken them.

Fortunately, it is possible to do more than break out in anger or break down with intolerable stress. It is possible to break through the barriers and the sources of pain into new adequacy, with coping skills necessary for life in our human state and our complicated world.

It is possible to look the paradox of suffering full in the face and discover that evil can be turned to good and sources of distress can be turned to modes of healing. The message of the Christian gospel is that the worst of times can be the seedbed for new and richer life, and the despair that often goes with suffering can be turned to a stimulus for creative change.

But the creative change cannot come by efforts to escape from responsibility. We cannot blame God for what happens in life and still develop the responsibility that leads to skills for managing what life brings. Recently, a mother spoke to one of us about the healing of her daughter, born blind as the result of her contracting German Measles during pregnancy. She said that if God did not heal her young daughter, she hoped the child would die because she could not stand the prospect of bringing up a blind child. When the child was in such desperate need for help, loving care and guidance, the mother was steeped in her self-pity so deeply that she lost sight of the child's needs, in her own self-interest. Here, the effort to blame God was used as an escape from reality, parental concern and personal responsibility.

Love burdens life. Love gives privileges but assesses the loving person with responsibility. Sometimes the burden becomes greater than the privileges and benefits of love. Then there is an effort to retreat from relationship. In New York recently, an ordinance was passed making dog owners responsible for certain aspects of canine behaviour. The next week over a hundred thousand dogs were turned in to the American Society for Prevention of Cruelty to Animals and dog pounds. Man's best friend may hold a tenuous place when the love given is balanced by an inconvenience. But if God is Love, the assuming of responsibility is essential to the fulfilled life, for life without love would be no life at all.

We enter life with the painful experience of birth. Often we end our earthly pilgrimage with times of acute distress. In our day, we can reduce many of the pains of life, but the fact of human suffering appears to be inescapable. We then are charged with a responsibility to cope with pain and suffering in as creative a way as possible. This calls for the best of our skills and the most perceptive of our insights. We have learned that the sharing of suffering tends to reduce it. A study of ten years' duration at Johns Hopkins Medical School of persons in intensive care units, cardiac care units and trauma units, shows conclusively that people who are abandoned in their illness have a poorer chance of survival than those who are surrounded with love, support and concern. The inter-relationships of life may cause suffering if poorly managed, but may relieve suffering when they produce tender love and care.

Meaningless suffering seems the hardest to bear. Speaking of his death-camp experience under Hitlerism, Viktor Frankl, the psychologist, said that the hardest suffering to cope with was that where no purpose could be found. Brutality for the sake of brutality, organized terror against life, or the acting out of sick emotions, were so meaningless and obscure that they were difficult to bear. When the purpose of the suffering is clear, it is not only bearable but may have a triumphant note about it. Implicit in the Christian view of life is this emphasis on shared suffering that has a redemptive quality about it.

Much personal growth begins at the point where disappointment occurs and life is reorganized to employ needed coping skills. Often acute deprivation is needed to change perspectives, to enrich the capacity for understanding and stimulate the human concerns that did not exist before suffering was encountered. Confronting barriers may change the course of life. Developing the skills to overcome barriers may not only reveal hidden strength but may refine its use.

Too often we drift along in carelessness, ignorance, and wilfulness towards our own destruction. A time of suffering may bring us to new understanding. We cannot blame God for the things in life for which we are responsible. Rather we must learn to accept blame ourselves where it is valid or project it on social processes where it is appropriate. Only then can we be in a position to use our skills to bring about useful change.

What have we been saying?

Suffering is a part of our human experience. It goes with a highly developed nervous system. It is enhanced by a well-developed social consciousness. If we take our suffering too personally, we become so immersed in it that it can drown us. But if we use our suffering to grow in personal responsibility, social purpose and inner adequacy, we will find that our suffering is transformed.

Instead of blaming God, we will find new security in the law and order of the universe with its dependability. We will learn the laws and live within their bounds and find new freedom and responsibility in doing so. We will then achieve the ability to transform suffering that seems purposeless to purposeful action. If the blind forces of the natural world assault us and we have no inner strength, then the suffering happens to us and we are helpless. If, however, we act out of a reserve of inner power and purpose, we encounter suffering and use it for our growth and increased understanding. The teaching and example of Jesus enrich our understanding of useful and purposive suffering, motivated by redemptive love. As long as we share the human predicament, we will know suffering. What we will do with our suffering will be conditioned by our effort to find and cope with its purpose skilfully. You alone can determine who is in charge of your life, your suffering or you.

13 The Gift of Hope

One of the most neglected words in the Christian vocabulary is 'hope'. Hope is confidence in the future, a faith that no matter how bad things seem, they will work out in the end. We need that conviction today more than at any time in recent history because our problems have accumulated and with this accumulation has come a prevailing cloud of pessimism, especially amongst intellectuals.

Let us analyze this word 'hope' and see if we can make it come alive and also explore some of the possible explanations of why some individuals are born optimists and others are born pessimists. A truly religious person seems full of hope and characteristically looks on the bright side of things. But if this is so we need to know why.

A radiant attitude of hopefulness is apparently not explainable either by reference to heredity or environment, as many other characteristics are. Brothers and sisters in the same family may be complete opposites in this respect. What then is the main explanation? Is it body chemistry, hormones, enzymes? One of the most promising fields of research is in endocrinology. It has been found that the pituitary and the glands it controls emit minute substances that cause individuals to fluctuate between optimism and pessimism, mania and depression, just as this same gland at the base of the skull emits a pain-killer that is said to be stronger than any pain-killer chemists have ever discovered. This may prove to be an important clue, but doubtless it is not the whole of the story because mental states may be due to other than chemical causes.

Many people seem to get this mental set early in life and it is hard to change. It is almost as if little pessimists and little optimists were born that way. Having had many graduate students one has come to know well, covering a period of fifty years of teaching, one becomes fascinated with the marked differences in them. It might be assumed that since they are supposedly rated on a common scale of competence, their characteristics would have striking resemblances, but this is not so. For example, here are two students with PhDs that one of us has known for fifty years. Student A has made a great deal of money as a writer on a variety of subjects, some of them popular stories, although, like the other man, he is a professional political scientist. From the moment he entered my classes, he was cynical, conceited, pessimistic, and abrasive. He expected the worst of human nature and was seldom disappointed. In some cases it might even be said that he helped it along. The only time he was really happy was when he was studying corruption in the boss-ridden politics of Chicago. He was the sort of person who curls up his lip whenever anyone says any-thing optimistic about human nature. Did his exaggerated egotism make him that way? Are all egotists pessimists because they are in-capable of seeing good in others?

Student B was almost the complete opposite of A. His father was a professor of religion at a church-related university in Southern America. He always smiled, had a contagious sense of humour, was more interested in others than in himself. When the United Nations was launched, Mr B joined at a low level, rose to the top, worked for it for thirty years until retiring and all this time, although he lived in India for many years where conditions in the large cities such as Calcutta are about as depressing as anything one ever observes, he never once lost his boundless optimism and idealism. The only time he ever laughed at others' foibles is when he laughed at his own stupidities or conceits.

What is now called personality science has begun to throw light on why some individuals in positions of power and responsibility are pessimist-cynics and others are suffused with hope. The two indivi-duals referred to above seem to have been that way since birth. The difference cannot be explained by differences in chemistry – although in some cases it may be a factor, but not very often. Nor can pessim-ism be explained by the hard circumstances of the individual's birth. Struggle, early in life, seems to motivate more individuals than it discourages. More important than either chemistry or environment is moral philosophy, as for two centuries at least, in Britain and abroad, it has been called.

During the late 1920s and early 1930s, one of the authors of this book had the opportunity to study some of the personages who exemplify the cheerful side of personality in public affairs. Professor Rosamund Thomas writes about some of these in her book, *The British Philosophy of Administration*, mentioned earlier. One of those the present author saw in action was Richard Burdon Haldane (later Viscount). He wrote books on philosophy, engineered reform of education in Britain, greatly enhanced the prestige of the British civil service. For fifty years or more, in all English-speaking countries, young people who discovered they had a public service motivation were attracted to Haldane instinctively. A contemporary of Haldane was Josiah Stamp (later Baron). He did a variety of things, from Treasury to running the LMS railway, to occupying a key position in Defence. He was hard-working, interested in others, hard-headed but practical, and invariably inspirational. Two leaders in the United States who resembled Haldane and Stamp were Walter Gifford of American Telephone and Telegraph and Owen D. Young, one of the early presidents of the General Electric Company. The latter was once seriously considered as a candidate for the presidency of the United States. What both had in common is that they were outstanding philosophers in the arena of public affairs.

What makes such outstanding individuals so valuable to society is that they build institutions that have durable qualities. They infuse them with life and vitality by contributing an institutional philosophy to the enterprise and setting up a succession system which tends to perpetuate forward-looking policies in its top leadership. The bedrock proposition is this: institutions do not survive unless they are grounded in moral philosophy. They must be honest, open, principled and responsive to the larger public interest. They cannot afford to do wrong or cut corners because the public invariably learns of such things, never forgets and punishes the transgressor in a variety of ways.

The four persons referred to happened to have outstanding personalities. They were warm, articulate, interested in others, possessed of what is commonly regarded as leadership qualities. But it may also happen that persons with hope in their hearts are quite reserved and not so colourful. An example of this is John Foster Dulles, who, as United States Secretary of State, made a great contribution to the founding of the United Nations. He was a man of strong principle. His principles were based almost entirely upon law and religion. He thought that the way peace would eventually come to the world would be through doctrines of fairness enforced by international agencies that were respected. And he felt so strongly and was so hopeful that even when his health began to fail, Dulles was still the optimist.

The opposite kind of person, the cynic-pessimist, has a philosophy of sorts, too. On close examination, however, this philosophy turns out to be little short of self-interest. At its worst, it is what in the vernacular we used to call dog eat dog. This philosophy, unfortunately, does its greatest harm when exponents of it head foreign offices. Without mentioning names, let us reduce to order the propositions on which the national interest doctrine is based. Everyone seeks power; the good things of life are limited; if my nation does not get a dominant share, some other nation will; the nation that most threatens one's self-interest therefore becomes 'the enemy'; all methods designed to promote a diplomacy of supremacy must be resorted to, including alliances; the final arbiter of advantage is war as a means of survival and maintaining one's power position in the world. This is called 'real-politik'. Actually, it is a prescription for eventual destruction. The only nation world public opinion likes has a moral personality.

Religion has much to do with whether the individual becomes a confirmed pessimist or whether he remains an optimist. Some large personages, like Eleanor Roosevelt, although they had many domestic tragedies, never faltered in their faith. One cannot explain such persons simply by saying that they had a great deal of patrician courage. They had that, too, but our observation is that courage alone is not enough. It must be deeply imbedded in faith or it cannot be maintained through every manner of adversity.

The word hope is found only once in the New Testament, but a dozen times in the Old. But Paul's statement, in his Letter to the Romans, is one of the pithiest statements in the entire Bible: if you would cooperate, the God of hope would fill your whole life with joy and peace and your life and outlook would become radiant with joy.

Hope is unlike some other key words in the Bible because it is so unambiguous. In the pattern of life, one is either a hopeful person or one is not. Moreover, unlike some other ideas, it is difficult to carry hopefulness to excess. A person can love his child and yet spoil him to the point of the child's raising havoc with everyone else. A person can have faith but be so lacking in love that he literally wants to destroy everyone who disagrees with him. But in the case of hope, the cheerfulness is catching and if at times hope turns to naivete, the naivete is easily corrected as one gains experience.

This leads to the contention of the so-called realists who have rejected idealism that if people would only be wholly intellectual and rigidly reject considerations of ethics and values from their discourse and behaviour, the world would no longer be imperilled. All too often this means equating logic with unadulterated self-interest. Or feeling that the only way one can profit is by getting the better of someone else. Hope, like everything worthwhile in religion, is a unity of intellect and feeling to produce sensitivity. Hope is part of a larger religious concept which may be called 'consciousness', or the transcendental interaction of life forces which tie people together in a radiant spirit and with their divine maker.

But it is not enough to recognize the centrality of hope: hope must also become operational. We need to be sure of what it consists before we can bring it to life and live it as individuals and as a nation.

There are four steps in making the doctrine of hope operational: decision, multiplier, deeds and radiance.

First, there must be decision. It is like deciding to be a religious person, a Christian, and then sticking to it. It is analogous with being 'saved' or 'reborn'. Also, decision requires will-power, a word that has almost completely dropped out of our modern vocabularies since the behaviourists became so intolerantly aggressive. Decision is the first essential step even for one of those fortunate persons who was born with the right endocrine glands.

Secondly, hope breeds hope. It is like compound interest. The more hope and faith one has, the more hope and faith grow. In Christian doctrine this is called 'grace'. If you work at it, God will help you. The harder you try, the more he will do for you. The scientists and the philosophers call this the 'multiplier' at work. So hope is not only an intellectual decision: it is the crops in the field that grow if one tends them.

Thirdly, hope depends upon works, deeds, becoming active in positive, unselfish ways. 'By their deeds shall you know them.' This is one of the respects in which Christianity differs most from certain other religions. It is not enough to sit under a tree and commit verses to memory or lose oneself in contemplation.

The final step is the radiation of hope that appears in some people's countenances. It is like a light that makes a person glow. Arnold Toynbee concluded that the ultimate test of a civilization's survival is this matter of radiance. Radiance results from being attuned, attuned to God and this transcendental thing called 'consciousness'. Radiance is possible only when the organism is unified, authentic and becomes so attractive that it has universal qualities which produce spontaneous admiration and respect. Respect for everything that God has created. A reverential attitude toward life. A feeling of being a part of, rather than superior to, which is the mark of the egoist and cynic. Arthur Koestler and all those who have probed deeply into creativity and genius find the secret of vitality and durability in a synthesis that radiates like a pure gem.

This is not to say that hope is all there is to the Christian religion. It is not, however, as much emphasized as it needs to be. Paul, in his Letter to the Corinthians, says there are three basic components of Christian character: faith, hope and love. The greatest of these is love. In the broad sense in which he uses the word 'love', one must, of course, agree. Even more persuasive is the interaction among these three. Religion is always an interaction and a unity and therefore no concept is so compelling that it can or should stand alone. Hope is fed intellectually by faith and is made operational by love. Or, putting it another way, faith is sometimes slow-growing and becomes stronger as one grows older. But without hope to sustain us, we might never develop the mature faiths that we all seek.

A more widespread feeling of hope would help to dispel the pessimism found in the Western world today. Hope is a solid confidence, a process, an evolution. Anyone can master it if he will. The result is a quiet self-confidence, a kind of innate power greater than that of rulers and billionaires. The person whose hope conquers all may lie dying but his or her faith is triumphant. Such a person may suffer the vicissitudes of Job and with every setback exhibit a more triumphant spirit.

So let us try to understand what hope is, what it consists of, how it develops step by step and how it can be recognized. Hope is fed intellectually by faith and is made operational by deeds and by the love that flows through them.

'We who have faith,' says Paul, in the Phillips translation of the New Testament, 'ought to shoulder the burden of the doubts and qualms of others and not just go our own sweet way. Our actions should mean the good of others – should help them to build up their characters. For all those words which were written long ago are meant to teach us today; when we read in the scriptures of the endurance of men and of all the help that God gave them in those days, we may be encouraged to go on hoping in our own time.'

14 Joy

A person who is attuned to God should be radiant and, if he radiates, he should be joyful. This should be true of religions universally, but it is especially to be expected in the case of Christianity, which is a religion of hope. Hope and joy are closely related, one being the cause and the other the expression.

There is no conventional definition of joy that satisfies one very well. It is said to be a pleasurable emotion due to a feeling of well-being; it comes when one is highly pleased. It is gladness, delight, an exultant spirit. It is a state of bliss, a feeling of felicity and, at best, it is paradise. All of these definitions have merit, but somehow they seem to skirt around the edge of the nucleus that ties them all together.

At its best, joy is a sustained feeling when spontaneously one senses that one's inner being is in harmony with those physical and psychic realities that give him a feeling of balance and completeness because they meet his need for unity. When the person's soul is in attunement with the oversoul, then the person feels secure and stimulated at the same time, and when this occurs, he presents a cheerful face to the world and feels like singing.

Music is perhaps the best, most natural expression of joy. Music of a certain kind, like 'The Hymn of Praise' from the Ninth Symphony of Beethoven, makes us cry with ecstasy or rise to the heights with aspiration, when nothing else does. Music is an integral part of religion and one of its highest manifestations.

This is not to suggest that there was ever a person who was joyful every day of his life, or even every hour of the day. Joy is like a peak experience. After lying latent for a while, it comes bubbling up. The

joyful person is therefore radiating with varying degrees of natural-
ness and felicity and at times he is not joyful at all. We are speaking,
therefore, of a general or predominant state of mind and spirit, because to assume that any person never fluctuates would be contrary
to all nature and all historical and behavioural knowledge we possess.

There would be more joy in the world of religion if we understood
more fully why joy is natural and why we should encourage it, rather
than to take on a long, sad face, as many religious people have sometimes thought fitting. Joy is not artificial. It is not an escape from the
dullness and disappointments of life. It is not escapism, if by that is
meant a recurring, almost perpetual state. It is what the French call
'joie de vivre'. It is élan, the face one characteristically turns towards
daily life, its disappointments and its successes. Joy is a native disposition which becomes more pronounced the more one believes in it
and encourages it.

I first began to sense the deeper significance of the term 'joy' when,
as a college student, I read a book by the English clergyman, L. P.
Jacks. His book is called *The Lost Radiance of the Christian Religion*
(1924). His thesis is that Christianity was meant to be a religion of
love and joy whereas it has become obsessed with suffering and sacrifice. L. P. Jacks does not object to the sacrifice theme, but his contention is that it should be secondary to and transcended by the sense
of love and compassion, the cheerful view of life, which Christ taught.
The person who has a long face and derives a masochistic satisfaction
out of suffering all his life can hardly be expected to have a cheerful
and infectious spirit. The joyful person can: he radiates his love, his
goodwill, his joy to be alive and to experience life to the full.

When my wife and I spent some time in India in 1964 (on a State
Department assignment, but in our spare time studying the Hindu
view of life), we stayed at a large religious compound where I gave a
lecture and where we visited with the saffron-robed monks. One of
them brought us a book he had authored called *The Christ We Adore*
and followed this up the morning we were due to leave Calcutta with
a 6 a.m. meeting on the veranda of our lodgings. In his book and in
his oral presentation, he argued that Christianity was originally the
religion of joy and that, as such, it deserves the support and admiration of all other religions. Later, however, it was beclouded by the

sadness of the crucifixion. The joyous element was lost and should be restored.

He made it clear that he was not suggesting that all Hindus should become Christians. Rather, his point was that all the major religions have certain dominant themes and that they all profit by appreciating what is different and desirable in other religions. He argued that the major religions have certain legends in common. The feature that sets Christianity apart from other religions, this monk continued, is the doctrine of joy. If the original intent of Christian teaching were followed consistently, people would become full of hope and full of joy because Jesus taught optimism, faith and a deep sense of cheerfulness which comes from being attuned to God.

This religious leader characterized the other religions: Buddhism teaches reflection and self-abnegation; Hinduism stresses one God with many voices and man's union with nature and all that God has created; Judaism is also monotheistic and stresses morals, ethics and duty to God's law; Mohammedism is a legal system similar to jurisprudence, but it also teaches universal principles and courtesy to strangers. But of all these religions, continued the monk, only Christianity is optimistic, upbeat and joyful. This joyful Christ, said he, is the one all religions should adore. And then turning to his guests, he said with an angelic smile, 'If you Christians would only act out the authentic version of Christianity, we would all join you.' By this time, it was 7 a.m. and my wife and I had to hasten to catch a plane. But we have never forgotten what the monk said and have read his book, *The Christ We Adore*, many times.

Theodore Parker Ferris, the former Episcopalian minister of Trinity Church, Boston, says in his published essays (*Selected Sermons*, Boston 1976) that Christian joy expresses itself in three ways: in the personality and life of Jesus himself; in his ministry and the record of what we know about him; and in the experience of those who become his disciples and experience the love and outgoing qualities he had. A Christian, Ferris concludes, is a person who communicates life and the life is that which was incarnate in Jesus.

Jesus' joyful, optimistic outlook is exemplified in his statement, 'Your sorrow shall be turned into joy'. Also, he came close to saying that joy is the essence of his teaching in these words, 'Enter thou into the joy of the Lord'. There are many ways, says Ferris, that Christ's joyful attitude may be observed in his personality and teaching: the very way he spoke and what he said; his calmness and his deep expressions of faith; his ability to look inside a person and to see what was good about outcasts and sinners; his compassion towards individuals and towards multitudes; his realization that often a person's intention is more significant than the outward form it takes; the decisiveness with which he faced death; and his devotion to humanity rather than to favoured individuals.

Ferris' admonition to Christians is particulary good: 'You may admire him, worship him, obey him, but if you do not enjoy him, you really do not know him.'

One of the best ways to judge whether Christianity is succeeding is to observe how many of its adherents are joyful. Ferris was being honest and realistic when he observed, 'There are always a few people in everyone's life in whom there is incomparable joy.' Only a few, yes, but note that Ferris says, 'incomparable', from which it may be deduced that most professed Christians have some degree of joyfulness in their personalities.

Why do we not make more progress towards the ideal of religion as joy? One reason has been mentioned: the competing tradition of sacrifice and suffering. Another is the theological doctrine that the body is evil and that man was born sinful. We get what we expect. A further factor is a stern censoriousness which assumes holiness on the part of the viewer and therefore characteristically misconstrues the intent of others. It sometimes results in a combination of authoritarianism and sanctimoniousness, which emerges as an attitude of superiority. And superiority, of course, is the antithesis of love and joy.

There are other reasons which are both historical and contemporary. The person who is willing to burn another at the stake because of the other's false doctrines is merely trying to avoid the erosion of what he considers the divine law, which must be enforced by every expedient. This is understandable, but such a zealot is hardly a joyful one. Then there are those who contend that hedonism is evil because it permits bodily enjoyment. These people do not understand the principle of balance, for it is only licentiousness and excess that are wrong and not the simple pleasures of daily living. But before one can see this and act consistently, one must recognize the unity of God and nature and the reason why balance is necessary to creativity, growth and renewal. It is the segmented, narrow zealot who is the main obstacle in the way of making joy the essence of religion. He claims to love, but he finds it easy to kill. He does not understand what Jesus meant by 'meekness' because his whole attitude is one of superiority. His idea of religion is a sanctimoniousness that expresses itself as meanness and superiority.

The rival doctrines of sacrifice and joy can be combined in the same personality. Altruistic sacrifice is a form of love. Sacrifice for the sake of sacrifice may become a pathology. Sacrifice is not a way of life, it is an incident in a total existence pervaded by joy. One should fight for higher causes, but keep a cheerful and tolerant attitude. To adjudge someone as wholly bad denotes a lack of understanding and compassion which cannot be squared with Christian doctrine. Our objective should be to become whole persons because only such persons are like God.

It is because we have misunderstood joy that we have been led into perversions of doctrine. Joy is not a superficial, evanescent thing. It has a deep quality, controlling all of one's life and personality. This kind of joy is like happiness, which is correspondence with nature. Joy is related to hope. Hope comes first. A person feels confidence, which allows him to be joyful, which causes him to be happy. This hope, this confidence, is rarely if ever achieved unless grounded in religious belief. But not just any religious belief; one whose principles are universal. Christianity was meant to be such a religion. And for some it always has been. Which are the Christians who impress one most with their Christian spirit? As Ferris has said, there will be some. There are many in small towns and in rural environments. Relatively fewer in large cities. In all such cases, these joyful persons have beliefs and faith in something that makes them hopeful, joyful and kind.

Those who, like Dean Inge and Harry Emerson Fosdick, and many others, believe that the essence of Christianity is joy, must certainly be right; and eventually their faith will be justified. Those who have always had a low opinion of human nature, like Thomas

117

Hobbes, the author of *Leviathan* (Fount 1976), were and are wrong. It is noble to suffer for a noble cause, but one should be cheerful about it. Masochism and self-pity are not Christian attitudes. If these simple insights and virtues were more widely observed throughout Christendom, there is no doubt that leaders of other religions, and not merely Hindu monks, would write about *The Christ We Adore*.

15 Peace

As long as there have been organized communities among humans, there has been concern for peace. People have long recognized the pain, suffering, devastation and group distress emanating from war-like behaviour. Most early forms of religion addressed themselves to this destructive form of human action. Yet never have the efforts to cope with war seemed adequate to confront the real problem. Early efforts were made to convert spears into pruning hooks and swords into plowshares. To turn aside from martial arts was set as a goal of those who would not learn war any more. Yet there continued to be wars and rumours of wars.

The high-water mark of the New Testament, the Sermon on the Mount, confronts the motivations that underlie warlike behaviour. To learn the ways and disciplines of love seems basic to a change in the root behaviour that causes wars. But the demands of this basic change in attitude have been so great that, although the blueprint for peace clearly exists, little has been built on it. Perhaps there are two reasons for this. First, the New Testament message has not been clearly understood. Second, peace has been seen primarily in negative terms, so the powerful dynamics necessary for its achievement have not been provided. It will be our task here to look at these reasons and explore what can be done now to realize the ancient hopes for peace.

In our day, the old problem exists with a new poignancy. A new dimension is added to the quest for peace. In the past, it has been a matter of relieving human suffering and finding new ways for changing human understanding. Now the stark reality is that our warlike potential could wipe humanity from the earth. This is the ultimate form of sacrilege, for, in destroying humanity, we would kill off the wonder of life at its highest level, the God-conscious creatures who alone of all beings are able to know and do the will of God. Our day, with its capacity for nuclear destruction, makes overkill a frightening possibility. Not only can we destroy every human ninety-six times, but much of plant and animal life as we now know it will be wiped out.

In the long, slow development of human personality, basic changes in attitude emerge slowly in an evolutionary process, rather than by great spurts of insight and new motivation. Yet the roots of this modification of attitude have been developing through many centuries. But the degree of self-understanding that is necessary to bring this modification to fulfilment has usually been obscured by social, economic and political forces that create a composite of mythic reality which seems to keep the needed solution out of reach. Self-interest seems so strong a motivation that self-destruction is camouflaged in a structure of negative, though sometimes noble, assumptions about life and death.

In our efforts to get beyond the assumptions about perverse and sinful humanity, it is essential to look for other and deeper causes of this non-rational and destructive component of humanity. It appears that warlike behaviour is a response to the heavy burden of consciousness – the battle-ground where instinctive forces are in active conflict with the elements of consciousness that would force humanity towards rational, disciplined and creative behaviour. Looked at in this light, we see that war violates our perceptions of God as love, truth and creative power. Yet the higher forms of consciousness are so essential to human motivation that these higher perceptions have to be recognized even in a perverted form. So, as a prelude to war, there must be propaganda, as a perversion of truth, hatred as a perversion of love and understanding, and destructive power as a perversion of the use of creative energy to enrich life.

Deeply rooted in life are primitive emotional forces that can be easily altered. When war comes, these emotional forces are the focal point of manipulative action by the power centres of group life. What are these deeply rooted and non-rational elements of being that can be used to generate warlike attitudes and actions? Basically there are five of these drives.

First, there is the 'stranger' response. The strange and unusual tend to trigger defensive responses. People of differing looks, colours, stances and characteristics stimulate some deep and sub-rational response. We tend to shy away. This response shows up early in childhood with hostile reactions to deformed or crippled persons. It is developed further in adult reactions to differing looks and attitudes, so that groups like the Ku Klux Klan in America and the National Front in Britain build on these feelings in generating action against Blacks, Jews and Catholics, with the more recent addition of Communists. Here, the threat to life seems to be related to the simple fact of being strange, different and unfamiliar.

Second, there is the security response to assumed threats. In nature, it is found in the actions of fish and birds when there is an intrusion of the nesting area. Fierce and courageous actions take place when threats occur; this is not limited to personal security, but has well developed social dimensions, as when flocks of little birds attack hawks or when hornets converge on an intruder who has stumbled over a nest. These security responses appear to be subthalmic activation of both glands and muscles in response to assumed danger.

Third, there is the reaction to the burden of consciousness, which in humans would usually lead to self-examination and more complete assessment of the total situation. These areas of higher awareness are later developments of mental activity and are not secure enough as yet to withstand the challenge of more primitive types of response. Under acute stress, people tend to retreat from reason and so the higher consciousness is apt to be subject to more impulsive and instinctual drives when threats to security exist.

The fourth appears to be deeply grooved patterns or habits of behaviour. When from early forms of primitive life certain ways of responding have existed, it seems easy to fall back into these patterns of response. Habits are not only personal but also social. Habits may manifest themselves in architecture and group life. So high places and fortified spots have been basic to human development. Such modes of thought and action continue even when the forms of group destructiveness have long grown beyond these ancient modes of life. Habits continue and seem to be replaced only with great difficulty.

The fifth is related to deeply rooted personality traits. The hunting instinct shows itself in many ways and the call to arms is often an activation of this response. Also the latent homosexuality that is a part of the transition period of adolescence may be reactivated or stimulated by the chance to escape from responsibility into another form of human contact. The camaraderie of paramilitary groups which continue long after the war has ended may well use this subconscious force.

These deeply rooted and powerful forces in personality must be confronted, examined and modified, if any significant movement toward more rational modes of behaviour is to be developed. Jung tried to identify a more gentle and compassionate factor in personality structure and referred to it as *animus* and *anima*. The assumption was that the female component of being was more gentle, loving and adaptive than the masculine component. But even this distinction seems uncertain, for recent history with Golda Meir and Indira Gandhi seems to indicate that political necessity and national security may overpower the more gentle components of personality. It seems that here we are coping with something more basic even than sex.

But that does not mean that it is impossible for people to develop modes of self-understanding and control that may effectively limit the more primitive drives of our natures. This may come about by using the old resources for new purposes. This seems to be the genius of the Sermon on the Mount, which would employ the powerful drives of our primitive natures for new and higher forms of creative action. So, to love one's enemies changes them from being enemies into new and understandable people. This new way can manifest itself in six basic attitudes that can be defined, developed and reinforced by new standards of group action.

First of these is a new perspective – humanity first. An awareness of a common plight and a common threat of destruction can move us away from small internecine ideas of conflict into a drive against the common threat of the destruction of humanity. We see some early manifestations of this attitude in tentative steps toward nuclear restraint, but national sovereignty still seems to have deep roots and continues to make its appeal to primitive emotions and small forms of group interest.

Second, there is the process of achieving identity with all humanity.

This carries the idea of humanity first to its next level of action, for here the effort is to perceive relationship in terms of the human endowment rather than the fear of the stranger. This calls for a different form of loyalty, motivation and discipline, but it will use the same basic human drives to meet larger human needs.

Third, there is the achieving of a capacity for communication, accompanied by a sharing that is like the old Quaker concept of 'the sense of the Meeting'. Here, not only new language ideas will be developed, but old language barriers with their emotional components will be replaced. This painful process is going on now as Arab and Jew seek to move beyond ancient barriers and Russia and America try to develop experimental ways of testing each others' emotions such as sincerity and human sensitivity.

The fourth is the necessity to re-examine and adjust to the facts of life. Mythology tends to create its own reality forms and conflicting mythologies tend to create artificial forms of reality perception. Facts and opinions have a way of becoming interchangeable under emotional stress. To keep basic facts in focus as opinions are formed may be essential to clear communication and realistic diplomatic action. It has long been observed that when factual communication breaks down, diplomacy gives way to military action. Clearly, a more skilful use of negotiating resources must be developed in order to avoid the retreat from reason and a return to reflexive action and primitive responses.

The fifth is the need to stand firm for alternative non-violent action even when and if reason fails. This may call for self-sacrifice for principle, rather than the kind of self-sacrifice that is so often a part of military action. This can become a well-developed reaction to failure of communication and adjustment. It may be a learned response to the need for a cooling off period before further efforts at rational negotiation take place.

The sixth is a form of religious affirmation, a willingness to stand firm in faith in the power of truth. This is far more than mere thinking in positive terms when negative action is urged. It is the assumption that deep within the consciousness there is an emerging sense of fulfilment when truth is served. Organically, people seem to be built to be comfortable with truth and uncomfortable with deceit. The polygraph is built on this assumption. When truth is violated, body systems, glands, muscles, skin, vascular and nervous systems respond so violently that it is clearly measurable. The adherence to truth is structural in the universe and in people. It is the willingness to support this universal principle that may well be the starting point for the achievement of a higher consciousness, personally and socially. It is the appeal to spiritual force.

Again, it seems to be in keeping with the basic idea of the New Testament and the Sermon on the Mount that this process of transforming basic life energy into spiritual power is essential to the achieving of both the inner kingdom and the outer kingdom where the spirit of God would be at home. However, the traditional response to this path has been to criticize it as visionary and impractical, to insist that it would not work. We have some partial illustrations from history.

In the Old Testament, there is the tentative expression of Hosea that love is better than hate and reconciliation is better than retribution. In the New Testament, there is the inspiring affirmation that the way of the cross is better than the way of the sword. The first three centuries of the Christian era are filled with the affirmations of the power of love and disciplined self-sacrifice to confront and change the greatest military power of the ancient world. Rome was impotent to cope with people who believed in something greater than the power to destroy. In the end, the power of the Roman Empire capitulated to the power of a spiritual force that had been let loose in the world. Painful martyrdom was finally triumphant over cruelty and destruction. The compromise with the state was at the expense of the state and a new order was instituted with a growing respect for the right of people to practice their faith freely.

We must face the fact that primitive emotions were always near the surface and could be easily activated. When the Cathari, the flower children of the Middle Ages, challenged the materialism and military power of the feudal-religious complex, they were brutally destroyed by the unmentioned crusade. Except for the Anabaptists and the Albigenses, who retreated into the hills, and the living witness of St Francis, this movement of love and peace was obliterated from the face of the earth. But the most brutal aspects of the Inquisition were finally overcome by reason and restraint and the witness of the victims has been preserved in literature, art and the emerging group consciousness found in a new tolerance of science and religion.

In Britain, the witness of the Quakers, who were willing to suffer for a cause, finally brought into being a reign of law that supplanted the reign of terror and opened a new era of British law. Cropped ears and skewered tongues were a painful price to pay, but war would have been even more destructive. William Penn worked so well with the Indians that his people were free from violence when neighbours were in active conflict with Indians. Quakers were hung on the gibbets of Boston Common until decent people were revolted and could no longer endure the process. And the Quakers who were sold into slavery would not be transported by New England seamen, in order that the practice was dropped. Almost singlehandedly, John Woolman assaulted slavery (but not the slave owners) in such a skilful manner that the conscience of the South was aroused so effectively that, had economic factors not entered the picture, the South would have rid itself of slavery in a few decades without the searing scars of civil war.

It may be argued that this is all right with sane people, but what can be done with a maniac like Adolf Hitler? Several years before Hitler came to power, the General Conference of the Methodist Church urged the rewriting of the punitive treaty of Versailles to show compassion for the plight of the innocent in Germany. This was not done, and the consequences were horrifying. The Jews, with a passive attitude of acceptance of persecution, let their group-paranoia keep them from taking a vigorous stand against Hitler's sick, racial policies. Yet, in Norway, where the teachers organized effectively against Quisling, he was unable to function and had to capitulate to their power of purpose. Even in the worst of circumstances, there can be creative alternatives when enough people work towards their goals with discipline and reason.

This Gandhi found in South Africa and in India. Satyagraha, the quiet and disciplined resistance to terror and injustice, made England impotent and India invincible. Martin Luther King mobilized the sense of justice in non-violent protest that broke through decades of repressive law and paid a great price, but the impact of his faith and conviction has been amplified in the lives of millions of his followers, black and white.

From many sources we have evidence of alternative forms of action in relation to peace. What can we conclude? We have looked at the frightening possibilities of our day for self-destruction. We have tried to look at the motivation for self-destructive action as a necessary prerequisite for affirmative action against war. We have assumed that the assaults on war in negative terms have been superficial and un-productive because the deeper roots in human nature have not been adequately assessed. We have examined the motivations proclaimed by the Sermon on the Mount. We have offered historical examples of the use of alternatives to violence and their consequences. We have looked at contemporary use of non-violent alternatives. Where are we to go now?

We can assume that we are running out of time to confront the full implications of modern war. We must decide quickly whether our loyalty is to people or things, neutron bombs or conciliation. We must decide which force we will support – resentment or forgiveness. This leads to a reassessment of our priorities in life. What is ultimately important for us?

Will we choose suffering and sacrifice with reason, or will we endure it with mindless destruction? Will we choose action with creative purpose, or with ruthless and irrational purposelessness? Will we give up on faith, or try to put our faith into action? Will we activate our spiritual resources, or will we in effect deny the power of the spirit to take relevant action in our time of greatest cultural threat? Will we acquiesce to the power of the primitive and destructive impulse in humanity, or will we commit ourselves to overcome evil with good?

Positive answers to questions of this nature will have an impact on our own behaviour. Instead of reacting to opportunities for creative action with passive submission, we can become patient, positive and progressive in thought and action. The approaches to peace in our day cannot be merely passive but must be active, dynamic and kinetic so that they draw all things to it.

The most exalted name for our master was Prince of Peace. At his birth, the angels chanted a song of peace. At his death, he symbolized the power of spiritual resource in coping with man's destructiveness. In a time when despair may stimulate a defeatist attitude, Jesus symbolizes a great hope. He invites us to learn a new and higher consciousness. Towards that end, all ingredients are now present in the world. We have the great need, the understanding of motivation and the hope of spiritual power in action. We are free to choose whether our personal investment will be in warlike action, or in the way of peaceful self-discipline and self-discovery. The crucial issue of our time is war or peace – the wiping of humanity from the face of the earth, or the learning of a new way for facing our international tensions. Will our personal answer be one of cowardly defeat or transcendent power? More than we may realize, we have the power and we are the answer.

16 The Search for the Real Jesus

Without doubt, the most influential figure in the history of the Western world is the man, Jesus of Nazareth. He has been the subject of more art and architecture than any other one person. Philosophical and theological speculation has whirled about his name and person. Writers in various fields, from Henri Barbusse, the communist, to Albert Schweitzer, the musician-surgeon, have explored the uniqueness of his influence. In between the extremes have been writers like Renan, Gilbert Murray, Edersheim and John Erskine, Jane Austin and Harry Emerson Fosdick, who share a common fascination with the amazing impact of Jesus on people and history.

Within this fascination lies an enigma, for the name of Jesus has been used as a magical symbol for many people in Christian history, at the same time that the person of Jesus has been a challenge to self-discovery and social responsibility for many others. How can the same person be used for such divergent purposes? How can Jesus be a symbol for retreat to primitive and magical thinking on the one hand and the challenge to the most audacious concept of the nature of God and man on the other? How can the enigmatic facts of history be resolved in the discovery of the real Jesus? The oft repeated search seems to invite continued efforts as each new generation provides for new and useful insights. So we make no excuse for our boldness in trying again to see more clearly the person who has inspired such loyalty and yet has been so confounding to historical perceptions.

We cannot hope to understand Jesus and his influence unless we try to fit his unique endowment as a person into a most unusual set of historical circumstances. Jesus was the product of important development factors in Jewish history. He confronted mankind at a critical juncture in history. Because his revelation is unique, he seems to precipitate important historical trends and at the same time challenge new movements of thought and action in the Western world. Yet, in one sense, he was not Western. His perception of reality melded ancient traditions and new moods in ways that have produced both perplexity and powerful stimulations.

At least seven important historical, social and personal processes must be kept in focus to see clearly who Jesus was and what his impact was and continues to be on humanity. From the proper relationship of these forces, we may be able to see more clearly the role of Jesus in Jewish history and the traditions of Christendom.

First, Jesus cannot be separated from the messianic hope of the Jewish people. Rooted in a variety of historical events, the Jewish people developed the idea that they were special to God. They were a chosen people and if they would be patient there would be a full realization of these hopes in a revelation of God's special interest in them, which would have not only religious but social and political significance. This hope was able to help the Jews to preserve their integrity and hold their national identity through perilous times. But there were unfortunate implications of this belief. It tended to fracture their grip on reality. In order to be true to their hope, they had to cling to a whole series of errors, not the least of which was the unfulfilled prophecies of the past. Efforts to preserve their special role in relationship to a tribal God made it difficult or impossible to relate to others as equals, so there was unending strife and inability to function in right relation to others and, at the same time, preserve the special role they claimed historically. So some Jewish authorities feel that the unfulfilled messianic hope has produced deep despair and other qualities of group life that make it difficult for Jews to function in the world. It may even be that this non-rational clinging to a hope of special relationship to God lies at the bottom of a long tradition of persecution that was endured, or even sought, as part of the price of faithfulness that would be ultimately fulfilled. Some Jewish leaders think that the messianic hope has been a tragic delusion for Jewish people.

Jesus was part of the history of those who desperately sought escape from the problems of their tradition by the coming of a deliverer.

He seemed to perceive the folly of such an unrealistic dream. Most of the recorded conversation of the gospel seems to indicate that he fought against the messianic concept and cast his strength behind an idea of responsible behaviour in response to the burdens of history rather than any claims of magic or easy escape from the burdens of history.

A second source of influence on the role in which Jesus was cast was the condition of the Jewish people at the time Jesus came on the scene. Subject to severe restriction by Roman rule, the Jewish state was divided among contending groups with differing purposes. Strong Hellenic influence was undermining traditions that had been deeply inculcated by Jewish history. Political groups were trying to preserve the past. Then, as now, Judaism was a centre for national life and culture as well as a religion. The Maccabees had revived Jewish hopes for a brief period but these had faded again into deep despair. Many had retreated to the desert or dispersed themselves throughout the empire. The rediscovery in recent times of the Qumran caves verifies the efforts to preserve the past and resist the disintegration of the Jewish nation.

Into this maelstrom of Jewish life, Jesus emerged with the probability that he had some relationship to the Dead Sea communities. But his emergence as a preacher of peace and spiritual disciplines was an affront to those who followed legalistic external practices as a verification of their loyalty to a tradition. Jesus chided those who made a show of externals and violated human justice and their responsibility to the universal need of humanity. His attitude towards Samaritans, for instance, was an affront to the Jewish community. But masses of people seemed moved by his message of hope that combined the best of the Hellenic logic with the finest of the Jewish concern about right relationship to God. But the efforts at modification and conciliation offended the politically strong segment of the Jewish community and he was removed from the scene by the joint action of Jewish and Roman leaders.

A third condition affecting the world into which Jesus was born was the deeply rooted conflict between the matriarchial influence and priestly role fostered by the patriarchal emphasis. Rooted back in pre-agrarian times, women had maintained the family and were the

131

centres of social stability, which later manifested itself in the growth of towns and cities. Men, as hunters, had lived in desert roamings and most of the great revelations had come in desert wanderings. Men regained their status in more stable cultural conditions by establishing a priestly class with primogeniture for men and servitude or a chattel status for women. This fitted well the rule of external law, but it did not fit so well the spiritual disciplines that Jesus taught. Here the primacy of the inner kingdom produced an instant form of spiritual equality. As Jesus pointed out, women and children are people too and entitled to the benefits of the kingdom. His vigorous challenge of the old ways of doing things was most pronounced at the point where he displaced both matriarchy and patriarchy as determinants of the nature of God. He revealed a God who was beyond sex distinctions. The energy characteristics of God are light, love, power, truth and spirit and they can be personalized by those who commit their lives to inner spiritual discipline, but they cannot be claimed by special privilege, for the natural order is subject to another and higher law than the Jewish tradition. The raw materials for the abundant life are available to all, for the sun and the rain are accessible to the wise and the foolish, the good and the evil.

This effort to move the ancient conflict above the level of traditional attitudes was an affront to the high priests who were the defenders of patriarchy. Perhaps more than any other one thing, this effort of Jesus to reveal a God above and beyond their trivial preoccupation with sexuality was a source of Jesus' downfall. Even now, Christendom has had difficulty catching up with Jesus and newspaper headlines continue to affirm that the priestly role has sexist connotations and women cannot fully share the disciplined spiritual life as it was taught by Jesus. The contemporary struggle of women for full rights in the human community amplifies for us the audacity of the teaching and practice of Jesus. It is little wonder that his ministry was short and that they tried to assassinate him after his first sermon.

A fourth condition that added to the uniqueness of his contribution was undoubtedly his own psychic endowment. Those who are highly gifted in perceptions into the nature of ultimate reality are often misunderstood and persecuted. Contemporary research in cosmic consciousness makes it clear that those who perceive with the clear vision of the mystic awareness are often mistrusted or the validity of their revelations discounted. It has been only in recent years, with the understanding of the integrative function of consciousness as it brings together the material, physical, artificial, paranormal, transpersonal and spiritual dimensions of reality, that we have understood the basis for revelation. Those psychic personalities that are able to open channels of perception into the oversoul or accumulated consciousness of the race are able to see clearly the truth that can set people free of their limitations and failures. Jesus was so highly endowed in his prophetic role that he moved ahead of normal human capacities for understanding by thousands of years and we have not yet caught up with the full meaning of the revelations that came from his life and teaching. Our day is better prepared to understand and accept the significance of psychic revelations because of the research in the nature and function of consciousness. Also, studies in anthropology make it clear that the psychic manifestations have been far more widespread than we have grasped with our limited historical insight. Jesus was far more than his contemporaries could perceive but for quite different reasons than his biographers have understood.

When we have brought together the messianic hope, the historical moment of the first century, the deeply rooted conflict between the priestly authority and the universal spiritual endowment, and confront these traditions with a psychic personality of Jesus' stature, it is easy to see why the full import of his revelation escaped his contemporaries and those whose loyalties claim to be centred on this unique person and his revelation.

That leads us to a fifth factor that we have to contemplate. Jesus was able to amalgamate in a unique way the solution to ancient problems and the challenge of the future. He did it by the uniqueness of his own person. The Christian religion has been largely a religion of a person, a purpose and a programme. Jesus represents the ultimate possibilities within the human being, yet his message is a constant challenge to his followers to fulfil their human possibilities by being and doing even greater things. The purpose is to develop the human potential to the place where it is fully using the resources of God for that more abundant life. The programme was set out in the Sermon on the Mount, where the powerful drives of life were used to fulfil spiritual purposes. It is easy for us to see from our perspective how this personal focus could lead to worship and a form of devotion that Jesus never asked for himself. Yet charismatic persons tend to elicit such a response. Even though Jesus was constantly emphasizing his humanity and denying his uniqueness, his contemporaries were so dazzled by his teaching and his action that they appeared to lose sight of the personal qualities of the one they were glorifying. So Jesus moved into history as quite a different person from the one of whom he sought to make his disciples aware. His revelation was so demanding for inner spiritual growth, that it was easier to make him unique and worship his uniqueness than it was to accept his revelation and follow his teaching.

In the sixth place, then, we must look at what history and tradition have done to the person and his revelation, the purpose he affirmed and the programme he sought to encourage. In a short time, the revelation of Jesus was adapted to the political and social exigencies of the time. The grandeur of his teachings was reduced to the cosmological and psychological perspectives that prevailed at the time. The Ptolmaic view from Egypt and the psychological view from Greece were melded in an institution that could cope better with magic and mystery than with a revelation of the truth that could set them free from cramped thinking and small-sized living. So Christendom turned its back on Jesus and the demands for responsible living that his revelation placed on his followers. Through the centuries, the person has been modified by artists, political figures and theologians until it would be difficult to relate Jesus to the tradition that uses his name and retreats from the burden of his revelation. Even the biblical record is so distorted that it is difficult to find the real Jesus in the revisions and editorial modifications that have prevailed.

In the seventh place, we look at our world and its effort to relate to Jesus and his revelation. We find confusion and a cacophony of voices that cry out in their disagreement. We find some who centre their religious thinking and practices around a mood of magic and the miraculous, even though Jesus was careful to avoid magic and denied the miraculous. We find others who would avoid all responsibility for spiritual growth by claiming that Jesus has done it all and there is no warrant for struggle to become sons of God for a magical historical event did it for them. Others have so identified Jesus with an institution that his spirit seems to be eternally imprisoned in an atmosphere he would probably reject. Others play word games with abstract concepts that effectively separate the name of Jesus from the person of Jesus. Powerful commercial enterprises exploit the name of Jesus for selfish purposes. As each generation seeks to find the true spirit of Jesus for its own time, so, also, each generation seems also to practice its own form of crucifixion.

Where in these conflicting traditions and differing modes of response to Jesus and his life can we find a revelation that can be relevant for our day? Where can we cut through the underbrush of history and find the person and the revelation that can strengthen the spirits of people and help them fulfil the promise of the New Testament in a more abundant life?

Some things can be done more easily than others. We know now why it was intolerable for persons of his time to confront the full impact of his revelation. So they made every effort to make him unique as their way to escape the burden of responsibility his revelation thrust upon them. In the Eastern milieu, it was easy to follow tradition and surround the beginnings and endings of life with the emphasis on a unique birth and a unique death. This was the pattern of at least twenty ancient ruling dynasties, the last of which was the Japanese emperor who was the direct descendent of the sun god. Because we reject the purpose of such efforts to create uniqueness, there is no reason to continue to accept the parenthesis within which their day tried to place his life. We can return freely to his expressed purpose.

It would make Jesus the ultimate hypocrite of history to have him claim a uniqueness that separated him from all the rest of mankind and then have him invite others to follow where he knew they could not go. He never asked to be worshipped, but he did ask to be followed in a way, a truth and a life that he sought to reveal to those who shared his personalizing relationship to the God who was equally available to all mankind, regardless of race, colour, or creed.

The respect for natural law as an important part of God's revelation was the theme of his first public sermon and also the temptations in the wilderness. Could the power of God be perverted by

135

those who would use nature for selfish purposes? Apparently he felt this was a hazard he would avoid at all personal cost.

Yet a major problem of our day is the careless disregard of our obligations to nature and natural law. We have built our culture on the use of crude and limited forms of energy and have disregarded the invitation to personalize the ultimate energy of creation. We have claimed to be God's elect, with the privilege of unlimited exploitation, when we have a common responsibility to the balances that are built into the world of nature. We do not manipulate the laws of nature and nature's God with impunity, for ultimately the immutable laws are not broken, but rather we break ourselves on them. That part of Jesus' revelation often goes a-begging.

When one listens to much of the preaching of our day, on radio, television or through the printed word, there appears to be a simplistic substitution of cheap salvation and magic in place of the strenuous and muscular religion of Jesus. The rationale seems to be that Jesus was strong in order that we can continue in our weakness. This seems to be a form of sacrilege that is hard to justify. This distortion seems possible only if Jesus is related to the old tribal gods that he rejected. This confusion comes from an undiscriminating approach to the scriptures that makes the whole Bible a valid revelation even though the developmental quality of it is so clearly obvious. But making the book magical fits the effort to make Jesus a worker of magic and this double error further removes the revelation of Jesus from the arena of human struggle and fulfilment.

However, with our perspective on history, our understanding of human possibilities and cosmological realities, we can set Jesus free from the clutches of a restraining history and the limitations of a distorted biblical record. Then history can serve its historical purpose and the scriptures can be used as they were meant to be used. The record of past human struggles will then be seen clearly with its historical values, its honest struggles, and we will be able to continue the processes of knowing God and being known of God without the millstones of the past hung about our necks. Then the name of Jesus and the person of Jesus will be brought together again and the long history of their unreasonable separation will be finished.

What then will be our relationship to God through Jesus? We

will be able to see his revelation as valid for our day with its new understanding of the energy of creation and the powers of human consciousness to be understood, and use this power for human growth and personal fulfilment. This may well be the first century in the history of Christendom that has had the mental equipment to understand and act upon the revelation of Jesus. When we can separate that revelation from the obfuscations of history, with their sordidness and misunderstanding, we may be set free to rise to the full stature of our transcendent and spiritual natures.

Perhaps there has not been a time in history when the equilibrium of destruction and re-creation stands so perfectly balanced. The abuse of crude power can produce the appalling possibility of multiple over-kill. The use of the power of God for accepted responsibility and disciplined response to nature can provide a time of human development that can move us a long way toward what Pierre Teilard calls the *omega* point, where creature and creator, where human and divine, the within-self and the beyond-self, will achieve a relationship that is marked by peace and compatability. Then there will be a movement beyond false values, false boundaries and false religion, to the implementation of the New Testament revelation.

Enlightened religion can make straight the way towards a new day in human affairs. A retreat to primitive motivations and unenlightened religion can continue the imbalances and the false values that pervert the teaching of Jesus. The time has come to end the sacrilege against that inspired and inspiring person of Jesus, whose unique endowment of psychic sensitivity and God-flooded consciousness would open a creative future for humankind if the restraints on that revelation could be broken. For the first time in history, we have both the resources and the needs for that breakthrough. Let us get on with it.

17 Towards a Theology of Relevance

Theology should be as dynamic as life itself. Too often in the past we have thought of theology as a structure of concepts rather than as a way of life. It has been thought of as the stuff of dusty books and ancient speculation that seems to be strangely irrelevant to our time and its needs. Can there be a theology that is contemporary and useful for our day? Can we create a personal theology that is essential to our life and our values?

In spite of what anyone may say, there is only one place where theological ideas flourish and that is within the sensitive spirit of the individual who seeks a creative relationship with ultimate cosmic reality. That is to say, there are two essential elements for a theology: a questing spirit in a human being and a relationship to a reality beyond the self. Systematic theology, historical theology, biblical theology, dogmatic theology, traditional theology, practical and impractical theology, are all superseded by personal theology, for ultimately that is the only place where a living relationship between creature and creator can be discovered. This is what emerges in the New Testament as the theology of the inner kingdom, truly a personal theology.

To put this in another way, this personal theology emerges where our concept of the soul, our psychology and our concept of the universe, our ultimate external reality, come into a working relationship. The working relationship is the individualized form of theology or meaning for life. Human history illustrates the meaning and verifies the value of this personal relationship of the self and the beyond-self.

Primitive man was so aware of his soul that he projected it upon all else in the outside world. He invested trees, plants, animals and birds with souls. His art was the creation of his resonance to external things. The Eskimo ivory carver would hold a walrus tusk in his hands and quietly talk with it. He would ask, 'Who are you, hiding in there?', or 'Will you let me help you out?' Only then would he be able to start carving, for he was cooperating with, rather than manipulating, his world. So it was that the Eskimos and the Indians found an intimate working relationship with their world and thus created a sound ecological relationship with the world of nature.

To be sure, they sometimes projected negative images and gave the thunder and lightning a personal vitality that led to personal sacrifice. Primitives tried to placate the souls of volcanoes by throwing sacrifices into their boiling depths. They danced rain dances to placate the angry gods who were withholding their rains. Some of this projection of personal feelings is reflected in early portions of the Old Testament where sacrifices, human and animal, were employed to placate nature and resolve guilt. God was considered to possess some of the more undesirable emotions of humans, such as anger and jealousy. But during long centuries of growth there was a change in this relationship between creature and creator. Anger was replaced by love, trust took the place of fear and creative relationship supplanted frenzied manipulation.

The New Testament made a great leap forward theologically. The New Testament idea of the nature of God is built around three concepts: the nature of the human being, the nature of the cosmic order and then, emerging from that, the concept of the nature of God.

The human being is richly endowed in order to achieve moral adequacy. He cannot blame God for failure, nor escape from the responsibility to use the resources of his endowment to build a more abundant life. To that end, he has been provided with all that is needed for personal responsibility and moral adequacy. Man's spiritual nature is made in God's image and the ultimate purpose of human life is to find the relationship with the beyond-self that makes it possible for the theology of the inner kingdom to be developed and fulfilled.

To that end, the human relates to a dependable universe which is the revelation of the nature of God. This universe is not capricious, or manipulable. It is an embodiment of the processes of cause and effect, or universal law and order. To try to make it anything else is inexcusable reductionism.

The nature of the cosmic order is reflected in the first recorded sermon of Jesus and the nature of his temptations and his response to them. In his first sermon, in Nazareth, he made it clear that the spirit of the Lord was upon him because of a relationship that existed. What he was and did was the basis for the response. Cause and effect were at work. There was no magic or mystery, for that would take the relationship out of the realm of the normal and would make it impossible for his followers to obey the command to follow him. He would not play impossible games with his followers. He would give them the assurance of a universe where cause and effect were inseparably bound.

This he elaborated in his temptations. First was the temptation to change molecular structure by changing stone into bread. He would not play fast and loose with the basic structure of the universe. He thought it sacred. Rather, he would adapt and discipline himself so that he could be resonant to both the personal needs of his hunger and the cosmic needs for ultimate dependability.

The second temptation had to do with violating the law of gravity and this he refused to do. He would not jump from the top of the temple and make a soft landing. That would be tempting God. Rather than be spectacular and seek superficial popular acceptance, he would take the more difficult but challenging route of working within the structure of cosmic law.

The third temptation was to use political manipulation to gain quick results. But he would not compromise in order to have half of mankind included because it would automatically lead to the exclusion of the other half. The revelation he would make had a universal application and he would not violate his trust in order to gain a partial but easy victory.

At each point, he affirmed his adherence to an uncompromising loyalty to the law and order of the universe. This is the essential dependability that all humanity has as its resource with which to work in creating a good life. In this process God does not have 'favourites'.

God's nature is committed to a cosmic justice that will not allow caprice or special privilege. The sun shines on the just and the unjust and the rain falls on the good and the evil. The individual's responsibility to work within the boundaries of cosmic order guarantees an unjudgmental relationship to God. The God of the New Testament is not angry or jealous but provides equal resources for life and guarantees full freedom to respond within the bounds of basic laws and orderliness.

This leads to a definition of the nature of God as the resource universally available. The New Testament speaks of God in irreducible terms, not as like anything else in creation, but rather as the basic energy of creation itself, physically, mentally and emotionally. The terms used indicate that God is love, God is light, God is power, God is spirit and God is truth. Each of these energy terms applies to a different area of the creative process. Truth is of the mind, love is of the emotions, spirit is of the soul, light is of creative cosmic energy and power is the essence of becoming. One cannot play games with these essential qualities of the universe and of God. One can learn to conform to law and use creatively the resources that are the revelation of God's nature.

This New Testament revelation of the nature of God and our relationship to this divine source of power for life was so demanding that it was almost immediately rejected. It demanded too much of the person in terms of discipline. It challenged both the Old Testament tradition and the Ptolemaic cosmology that was universally accepted. It also took away the main tool of the priestly class, whose authority was based on their assumed power to manipulate the deity and, by indirection, the cosmic order.

Rather than meet the obligations implicit in this revelation of the nature of God, it was summarily rejected. St Paul, who had no first-hand knowledge of Jesus and his revelation and was sorely troubled by personal problems that led him to see through a glass darkly, led the movement towards compromise. Rather than being those who preserved the sacredness of the great revelation, the confused and conflicting disciples furthered a retreat from it and the organized church enhanced its own power by moving towards a claimed role as cosmic manipulator.

The course of the history of Christendom has made it more difficult to focus on the original revelation. The nature of the person and the role of Jesus have been obscured. His life has been bracketed by untenable and irrelevant miracles, even though Jesus made it clear he did not believe in miracles himself. He has been made so unique that the significance of his revelation has been distorted and, for all practical purposes, destroyed. His invitation to follow him and work through his revelation has been made practically meaningless by using his assumed uniqueness to avoid responsibility for confronting the meaning of his revelation. For that reason, most of the impact of his life and teaching has been destroyed and the history of Christendom has been marked by denial, failure and rejection of the revelation in favour of a reductionist facsimile.

For centuries, the substitute for the true New Testament theology has been promoted by an institution that has emphasized the manipulative and has sought self-preservation of its perversion rather than a clear interpretation of the teachings of Jesus. If theology is to become relevant for our day, we must go back to the origins and see them clearly enough to interpret them to our day. This we can do for our time may well be the first century in history that has a psychology and a cosmology that can understand and value what Jesus revealed.

Contemporary humanistic or consciousness psychology looks at the spiritual endowment of human beings from an unlimited perspective and sees the validity of the New Testament revelation. Contemporary energy physics looks at the nature of ultimate reality and resonates to the concept of the nature of God as the basic source of energy in all creation. We have the raw materials to implement a theology of personal fulfilment for the first time in history. The basic question is, how can we make it relevant for mankind in our day?

Unfortunately, the main religious movements of today are elaborations of the ancient fallacies and denials. The popular evangelists emphasize simplistic manipulation as an escape from basic responsibility. Too often, the charismatics practice an easy escape from reality into a private encounter with a small-sized God who becomes their cosmic errand-boy. The main-line churches still proclaim a theology of irrelevance and then wonder why they have been losing influence.

One need only turn on the radio or television to be subject to a flood of religious broadcasting that projects illusion and delusion, so that the main thrust of popular religion in our day is a vulgar parody of the strenuous and muscular revelation that comes through the ideas and actions of Jesus. As long as the manipulative use of theology is employed for personal profit and trivial self-interest, it will be difficult to encourage a return to the basic truth of the New Testament revelation. But that is no excuse for not trying.

What can we do to make theology relevant for our day? How can we make the New Testament revelation come to life in this time of psychological and cosmological opportunity? How can we encourage a theology that is free from illusion and delusion?

The creative use of theology must have at least five ingredients. First would be personal responsibility for making the revelation relevant. This calls for the courage to move beyond a small-sized concept of God. The cosmic scapegoat has not served us well, for it has destroyed our sense of obligation for bringing theology to life within ourselves. As long as we can blame God for what happens in life and in the world, we will not develop our own courage and spiritual muscle.

Second, we need a discipline that faces our obligations to the revelation of Jesus and its theology of relevance with a courage willing to reject the inadequacies of the past. We can no longer retreat into a cosy, but false, view of God's nature. We cannot act as if God is playing games with us. We cannot say, 'Oh God, I will be nice to you if you will be nice to me.' It is not that kind of universe and we fool only ourselves if that is what we try to make it. We will have to be disciplined enough to reject reductionist religion in the name of a clearer sense of obligation that emerges from self-discipline.

Third, we will have to find the inspiration that can warm our intellectual perceptions. Our faith is like a three-legged stool. It must provide balance and stability. Beliefs are the way the mind deals with faith. Convictions are the emotional dimension of faith. Action is the physical acting out of faith. Beliefs without conviction or action are sterile. Convictions without balanced perceptions and sound reason can lead to tragedy. Actions that are not secured in proper thoughts and feelings may easily lead one astray. A sound faith can inspire a person to accept responsibility and develop discipline.

Fourth, there is the need for implementation. Sound theology that is not put to work serves no purpose. Theological perceptions must be imbedded in science, economics, politics and the social structure of life for them to become relevant. Until we can bring our theological perceptions to life in practical affairs, they might as well be confined to ancient and dusty tomes.

Fifth, a relevant theology has at its core a reciprocal relationship. The theology that enriches and fulfils life wins the support that makes the theology more valid. It becomes a self-verifying process, where life enriches faith as faith enriches life. Then a contagious development takes place and the personal and social fulfilment breed hope, endurance and character, and these qualities make it possible for the fruits of faith to be enmeshed with the tasks of building a more abundant personal and social life.

These five ingredients can make it possible for a relevant and useful theology to be applied to life and society. The New Testament offers these resources for building a theology of the inner kingdom, a personal theology with social dimensions.

In a time of personal, social and national crises, we need the best resources for coping with the problems of life. Most life crises are essentially theological, a quest for adequate meaning and resources. When we trivialize theology, we also trivialize life. Small gods serve little purposes. Little men foster the use of small gods. Jesus challenged mankind to grow to the place where it could be at home in the universe, able to rise to its full stature as spiritual beings. We have too often sold ourselves short spiritually and have had to pay the consequences in human pettiness and social stress that lead to divisiveness and destruction.

With the clearer revelation of the meaning of the New Testament that our contemporary perceptions make possible, we no longer can be satisfied with the small gods that lead to puny faith and trivial action. Rather, we can bring together our best understanding of the nature of the human consciousness and our best perception of the laws and resources of the universe within which we exist, to achieve an interrelationship that is the product of responsibility, discipline and inspiration, that lead to implementation and personal and social fulfilment. We have the makings of a theology that is relevant to the needs of our day. Only we can determine whether or not it will be employed for the creative tasks our day thrusts upon us.